PANTRY GENIUS

Anna Berrill is a food writer and editor based in London. She is a regular contributor to *Feast*, the *Guardian*'s Saturday food magazine and writes their weekly Kitchen Aide column. She has previously worked for *Waitrose Food*, *Jamie Magazine*, *Red*, *Homes & Gardens*, *Food & Travel*, the *Huffington Post*, *Healthy*, and *Decanter*. She also appeared on Radio 4's *The Food Programme*, as well as the *Guardian*'s *Today in Focus* podcast. This experience has given her a keen eye for food trends, what people are cooking, and how to get the best out of each ingredient.

Agnieszka Więckowska is a Polish illustrator and graphic designer based in Wrocław with 15 years' experience in the creative industry. She focuses on creating illustrations for publishers, institutions, and brands, including Adobe, Kinley and Accor. szarobiuro.eu

Anna Berrill

PANTRY GENIUS

200 CLEVER RECIPES TO TRANSFORM YOUR FORGOTTEN INGREDIENTS

Illustrations Agnieszka Więckowska

Skittledog

Contents

Secrets of the pantry	6
Getting organized	9
The shopping list	10
Sriracha	12
Sweet corn	16
Miso	21
Tahini	24
Canned tomatoes	29
Butter beans	32
Canned pineapple	37
Artichokes	41
Cannellini beans	44
Canned sardines	49
Polenta	52
Roasted red bell peppers	57
Chickpeas	60
Harissa	65
Bread crumbs	68
Mango chutney	73
Dried mushrooms	76
Dark chocolate	81
Oats	84
Green lentils	89

Honey	92
Coconut milk	97
Preserved lemons	100
Nuts and seeds	105
Preserved cherries	108
Peanut butter	113
Kimchi	117
Anchovies	120
Noodles	125
Mayonnaise	128
Canned tuna	133
Black beans	136
Mustard	140
Rice	145
Pearl barley	148
Couscous	153
Chickpea flour	156
Red split lentils	161
Capers	165
Pomegranate molasses	168
Recipe index	172
Acknowledgments	176

Secrets of the pantry

Everyone has *that* shelf in their pantry; you know the one—where the cans, jars, and packages that grease the wheels of your everyday cooking sit front and center, while others are relegated to the back, crying out for you to finally do something with them.

There will be no two pantries that are the same; what I might consider essential (miso, peanut butter, chickpeas) will be different to you. That said, I think we can all agree there are some ingredients that give you the power to regularly rustle up a quick dinner: canned tomatoes turned into a pasta sauce with olives, maybe capers, and/or an anchovy fillet or two—whereas others continue to lurk, after being purchased for a single recipe. And it's here where this book, I hope, will help, showing how to make breakfasts, lunches, dinners, and snacks using the ingredients you already have to hand.

Growing up in London, I was lucky to be exposed to different cuisines and cultures: dals, spiced pumpkin, and a medley of chickpeas, kidney beans, and chunks of potatoes in a yogurty sauce from the local Afghan restaurant; Chinese dumplings and chow mein or a trip to the fish and chip shop were the go-to choices whenever the option for a takeout arose. All of this has influenced the way I like to cook and eat, but these recipes are by no means traditional ones. I've learned that there is a fine line between basic and

brilliant, and the secret is often spices, sauces, pastes, and condiments, so be sure to harness these, too. A tablespoon of miso, for example, will add layers of depth to soups, spaghetti, roasted tomatoes, and cookies, while I can't get enough of harissa for swirling through soups or root veg. Pickles and ferments (think kimchi and sauerkraut) play well with grilled cheese and so much more, while most things can be vastly improved with a squeeze of lemon or lime juice. A core set of spices will allow you to achieve maximum flavor but with minimum fuss.

Of course, dried ingredients and canned food can't always work alone. They need a few fresh things, be it fruit, vegetables, meat, fish, cheese, eggs, or herbs, to really sing. While this isn't a vegetarian book, a large proportion of the recipes are vegetable-forward as this is the way I believe we should be (or at least try to be) eating for sustainability—a benefit is that this often works out to be more affordable.

While many of these recipes can be whipped up midweek— peanut noodles with smacked cucumber (page 115), cacio e pepe butter beans (page 34), lemon and green olive spaghetti (page 102)—you can also lean on your pantry come the weekend, when friends and family need feeding: artichoke skillet pie (page 42), fish parcels with lemon and capers (page 167), or whipped tahini with squash and pine nuts (page 27), while no one ever turned down a harissa cheese straw (page 67) or miso mushroom sausage roll (page 70). Breakfasts, lunches, and bakes are also covered, from carrot cake overnight oats (page 86), to honey roast grape and goat cheese toast (page 95), and cherry and basil friands (page 110).

Getting organized

My pantry shelves flit between being an ode to disorganization and something more ordered. When it falls into the former camp, it really helps to do an audit then make a game plan.

NOT ALL PANTRIES ARE CREATED EQUAL

Getting a grip on the contents of your pantry will be made much more achievable if your ingredients are stored in glass stackable containers or jars—I'm a big fan of these, and not simply because they look good. They keep things fresh, but they also allow you to actually see what you've got, meaning you're more likely to use it all up. Make sure you write down what's inside your containers and any expiration dates—you think you'll remember, but you won't, especially when it comes to flours and spices. You could go one step further and categorize your containers, but the key thing is to have visibility so you can easily formulate a pantry-raid dinner plan.

BEYOND THE PANTRY

Think of your freezer as an extension of your pantry. Stock up on bags of frozen peas, sweet corn, and—a personal favorite—spinach, and freeze any surplus veg, such as onions, leeks, squash, chiles, and grated ginger. (The holy trinity of garlic, ginger, and chile should never be underestimated, especially when predominantly pantry ingredients are involved.) In the same vein, herbs can be chopped, popped into bags or containers, and frozen, ready to pep up curries, stews, and soups, which, in turn, are all prime candidates for batch cooking and filling your freezer with. This will not only help reduce food waste but make future dinners a whole lot easier. The roast red pepper and lentil soup (page 163) and cauliflower, carrot, and spinach dal (page 98) are good places to start, plus you'll want a stash of chocolate, miso, and pecan cookies (page 22) in there, too.

The shopping list

You don't necessarily need a recipe for dinner—but you do need to have the staple supplies. Having these essentials in stock will mean there is always something you can cook up.

COVER THE BASICS

There are some essential items that should feature on your shopping list: canned tomatoes, beans, chickpeas, bouillon, pasta, noodles, rice, a few dried herbs and spices, plus some nuts and seeds for texture. What follows depends on your tastes: coconut milk, peanut butter, harissa, miso, mustard, tahini, and canned fish. For those regular stars, buying in bulk can be a cost-effective strategy, especially when it comes to things like rice. If space and budget allow, a few oils and vinegars will keep things interesting: olive oil, a neutral oil, toasted sesame oil, wine or apple cider vinegar and balsamic vinegar, plus rice vinegar, soy sauce, and maybe fish sauce. A wide variety of ingredients are available in most supermarkets but do seek out local specialty stores and Asian stores for condiments and sauces to pack in the flavor (as well as provide inspiration).

AVOIDING FOOD WASTE

It may sound boring but making a meal plan for the week saves you time and results in far less food waste. Just like pantries, refrigerators can descend into chaos, so rearrange your shelves regularly to ensure produce nearing their use-by dates are top priority. Surplus fruit and veg can be turned into chutneys, pickles, and preserves to enliven a whole host of meals; stir salad leaves that have seen better days through soups and stews; whizz the ends of loaves into bread crumbs ready to add texture to pasta dishes or gratins; chuck surplus nuts into a food processor for pesto or toast and chop to sprinkle over salads. Essentially, be resourceful, and when it comes to pantry ingredients, don't cook more than you need.

A FEW OF MY FAVORITE THINGS

I am not one for too many kitchen gadgets, but there are a few items that just make life easier. First, **KNIVES**, aka the most important tool in any kitchen; all you need is a good chef's knife (as large as you feel comfortable holding), a petty knife/small utility knife (for taking the tops off tomatoes, for example) or paring knife, plus a bread knife, for obvious reasons. **MICROPLANE ZESTERS** are my go-to for fine zest, but are also great for garlic, ginger, cheese, and nutmeg. An **IMMERSION BLENDER** is essential for soups, marinades, sauces, and curry pastes, plus a **PESTLE AND MORTAR** for crushing spices. You'll need a **FOOD PROCESSOR** for pulsing pesto, grinding nuts and seeds, and finely chopping veg. **SILICONE SPATULAS** are useful for getting every last thing out of the pan as is a **SILICONE PASTRY BRUSH** for applying an egg wash or oil over vegetables for roasting. Of course, you've then got **MEASURING SPOONS**, **CUPS**, a few **MIXING BOWLS,** and **PANS** (of which you only really need three in your arsenal: a cast-iron skillet, a casserole dish, and a smaller pan), but see how you cook and equip accordingly. You'll need less than you think.

Sriracha

Originating from Thailand, this fiery, tangy sauce is made from a paste of chiles, garlic, vinegar, salt, and sugar. It's not hard to see why sriracha has reached cult status, either. Yes, a drizzle can bring pretty much any dish to life (particularly when eggs are involved) but a squirt can also elevate glazes for chicken wings, rice dishes, and dipping sauces destined to sit alongside the likes of shrimp—or even mix into a Bloody Mary.

PAIRS WITH	Chicken, pork, shrimp, crab, potato, pumpkin, cauliflower, sprouting broccoli, asparagus, avocado, lime, egg, tofu, peanuts, and popcorn.
TRANSFORM	Add a kick to a cocktail sauce by combining sriracha, ketchup, horseradish, Worcestershire sauce, and lemon juice. Serve with oysters.
HACK	For a sweet and spicy snack, try roasting cashews or almonds with sriracha, maple syrup, and salt.

Sriracha baked salmon

1 tbsp. sesame oil
1 tbsp. soy sauce
1 tbsp. sriracha
1 tbsp. white miso
1 garlic clove, crushed
Pinch of sugar
2 skinless salmon fillets
(about 8 oz.)

**A simple, sweet, and savory salmon that partners well with
a peppery green salad.**

Preheat the oven to 350°F. In a bowl, combine the oil, soy, sriracha,
miso, garlic, and sugar to make a glaze. Put the salmon fillets on a
baking sheet, brush with half the glaze, then flip the fish over and
brush the other side with the remaining glaze. Cover and put in the
refrigerator for 1 hour. Bake for 15-17 minutes, until the salmon is
cooked and easily flakes away with a fork. Serves 2.

Sriracha sprouts

3½ cups Brussels sprouts,
halved
Drizzle of olive oil
2 tsp. golden honey
1 tsp. sriracha
Quarter of a lime, juiced
Sesame seeds, to serve

**When roasted, sprouts take on an almost nutty flavor, which
makes them a great candidate for pairing with fiery sriracha.**

Preheat the oven to 400°F. Toss the sprouts with a little oil, salt, and
pepper, then tip into a baking dish and roast for 20 minutes, turning
halfway through cooking, until tender and golden at the edges.
Meanwhile, whisk together the honey, sriracha, and lime juice.
Tip over the sprouts and toss to coat, then return to the oven for 10
minutes. Serve sprinkled with sesame seeds. Serves 2.

Sriracha mayo

1 garlic clove, minced
⅜ cup mayonnaise
1 tbsp. sriracha
1 tbsp. lemon juice
Pinch of salt

**Two condiments combine to achieve creamy, tangy,
garlicky greatness.**

Put all the ingredients in a small bowl and combine. Serves 4.

Sriracha pickled cucumbers

A quick pickle to stuff inside burgers or serve with rice.

1 cucumber
1 tsp. salt
1 tbsp. white wine vinegar
1 tsp. superfine sugar
1 tbsp. sriracha
Handful dill, chopped

Finely slice the cucumber using a peeler or knife. Transfer to a colander, toss with the salt, and set aside for 20 minutes. Squeeze out any water, then pat dry with kitchen towel. Transfer the cucumber to a bowl and toss with the vinegar, sugar, sriracha, and dill. Taste and add more sugar if need be. Serves 4-6.

Sriracha garlic bread

Warm, buttery, and with a bit of bite from the sriracha. You could add some shredded cheese, but I don't think it's needed.

¼ cup unsalted butter, softened
2 garlic cloves, crushed
2 tbsp. sriracha
3 scallions, chopped
2 tbsp. chopped parsley
1 baguette

Preheat the oven to 375°C. In a small bowl, combine the butter, garlic, sriracha, scallions, and parsley until you have a paste. Put the baguette on a large sheet of aluminum foil and make even diagonal slices all along the bread (but don't cut all the way through). Spread the butter between each slice, then wrap it up in the foil. Bake for 20 minutes, open the foil and return to the oven for 5 minutes to crisp up. Serves 4.

Sweet corn

Growing up, sweet corn meant two things: the jolly Green Giant and tuna and sweet corn pasta. These days, corn on the cob drowned in butter is hard to beat, but the season is brief, so it is wise not to underestimate the canned stuff. Preserved at their peak, budget-friendly, and ready to eat year-round, the canned kernels can bulk out and bring instant sweetness to weekday stalwarts, such as soups, pastas, and the ever-customizable fritter, as well as weekend pies, tacos, and burgers. Sweet corn can also shine in numerous side dishes, from salsa to chaat to corn bread, so it's high time we appreciated its culinary merits.

PAIR WITH	Mexican and Asian flavors, sweet potato, chile, lime, coconut, lemongrass, paprika, bacon, chicken, haddock, sea bream, crab, and ricotta.
SWAP	Frozen sweet corn is also handy and can be used in place of the canned stuff—just thaw it in warm water before using.
HACK	Blitz the kernels in a food processor to bring flavor and texture to soups.

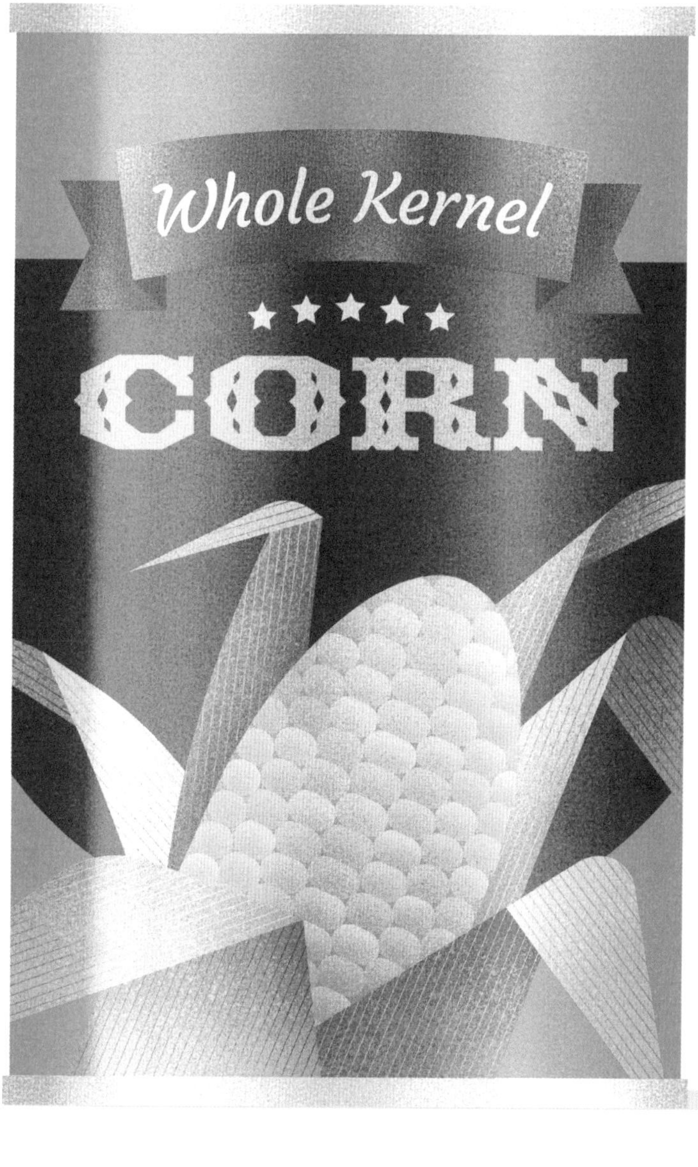
Whole Kernel
CORN

Sweet corn, spinach, and feta phyllo triangles

1 tbsp. olive oil

1 onion, finely chopped

5 cups spinach

¾ cup canned sweet corn, drained

⅔ cup feta, crumbled

Small bunch mint, chopped

1 lemon, zested and juiced

1 package phyllo dough

Melted butter, for brushing

These phyllo triangles are equally good straight from the oven with a sweet chili sauce as they are the next day for lunch.

Heat the oil in a saucepan and fry the onion for about 10 minutes, until soft. Add the spinach and continue cooking until wilted and any liquid has evaporated. Tip into a bowl with the sweet corn, crumbled feta, mint, the zest and juice of the lemon, and season well.

Preheat the oven to 375°F. Lay a sheet of phyllo dough on a countertop with the short end facing you and cut into three strips. Brush the edges with a little melted butter, add 1 generous tsp. of the sweet corn mix to the top corner of each strip, and fold diagonally to make a triangle. Continue to fold over down the length of the dough, brushing with more melted butter to help it stick. Repeat until you have used up all the filling. Transfer the triangles to a lined baking sheet, brush with more melted butter, and bake until golden, about 20 minutes. Makes about 24 triangles.

Sweet corn and black bean nachos

1 tbsp. oil

2 garlic cloves, finely chopped

Small bunch cilantro

1 can (14½ oz.) chopped tomatoes

1 can (15 oz.) black beans, drained and rinsed

2½ cups canned sweet corn, drained

1 red onion, thinly sliced

2 tbsp. red wine vinegar

7 oz. tortilla chips

1 cup shredded Cheddar

1 avocado, diced

Sour cream, to serve

1 lime, quartered

The ultimate sharing dish, dig into these nachos straight from the (cooled) pan.

Heat the oil in a saucepan, add the garlic and a handful of chopped cilantro stalks, and fry for a couple of minutes. Stir in the chopped tomatoes, black beans, and sweet corn. Add 3 tablespoons water, and simmer for 15-20 minutes until reduced. In a bowl, mix the onion, vinegar, and a pinch of salt and pepper.

Preheat the oven to 425°F. Spread out the tortilla chips in an ovenproof dish and top with the bean mix. Sprinkle with shredded Cheddar and bake until the cheese has melted, about 10 minutes. Remove from the oven and top with the avocado, the onion mix, some cilantro leaves, and sour cream. Serve with a wedge of lime. Serves 4.

Sweet corn drop scones

Perfect for brunch, eaten with eggs, crispy bacon, or avocado.

¾ cup whole-wheat flour
½ tsp. baking powder
3 eggs, beaten
Big handful cilantro, chopped
Bunch scallions, chopped
1¾ cups canned sweet
   corn, drained
Drizzle of oil

Mix the flour, baking powder, and beaten eggs together in a bowl, then fold in the cilantro, scallions, and sweet corn, and season. Heat a little oil in a skillet and cook tbsp. of the mix until golden brown on the base, about 2–3 minutes, then flip and cook on the other side until golden brown. Makes about 6 drop scones.

Sweet corn slaw

A solid side for grilled meats that's quick to pull together.

Half a white cabbage
1 red onion
Handful radishes
1 can (8¾ oz.) sweet corn,
   drained
1 red chile, finely chopped
Handful cilantro
2 tbsp. yogurt
Half a lime, zested
   and juiced
Squirt of golden honey

Shred the white cabbage, red onion, and radishes into a large bowl. Add the drained sweet corn, red chile, and cilantro, and combine. In a separate bowl, combine the yogurt with the lime zest and juice, honey, and some seasoning. Tip into the slaw and mix until everything is evenly coated. Serves 6, as a side.

Corn bread with roast tomatoes

This is best served in wedges, with the tomatoes spooned on top, so the corn bread soaks up all the garlicky juices.

3½ cups cherry tomatoes
2 garlic cloves, chopped
Drizzle of olive oil
1½ cups canned sweet corn,
   drained
4½ tbsp. milk
⅔ cup yogurt
2 eggs
½ cup shredded Cheddar
Pinch of red pepper flakes
½ cup + 1 tbsp. all-purpose
   flour
¾ cup quick-cook corn
   meal
2 tsp. baking powder
3 tbsp. + 2 tsp. butter

First, halve the tomatoes and put in a roasting dish. Top with the garlic cloves, a drizzle of olive oil, and some salt and pepper. Roast for 40 minutes until golden. Meanwhile, put the drained sweet corn in a food processor, blitz until coarse, then transfer to a bowl. Mix in the milk, yogurt, eggs, most of the Cheddar (reserve a handful for topping), and the red pepper flakes.

Preheat the oven to 425°F. In a separate bowl, combine the all-purpose flour, corn meal, and baking powder. Tip into the sweet corn mix, season with salt and pepper, and stir. In an ovenproof pan, melt the butter, tip into the batter, and combine. Tip the lot back into the hot pan, smooth over, top with the reserved cheese, and bake for 25 minutes, until a toothpick inserted into the center comes out clean. Leave to rest for 5 minutes, then slice and serve with the tomatoes on top. Serves 6.

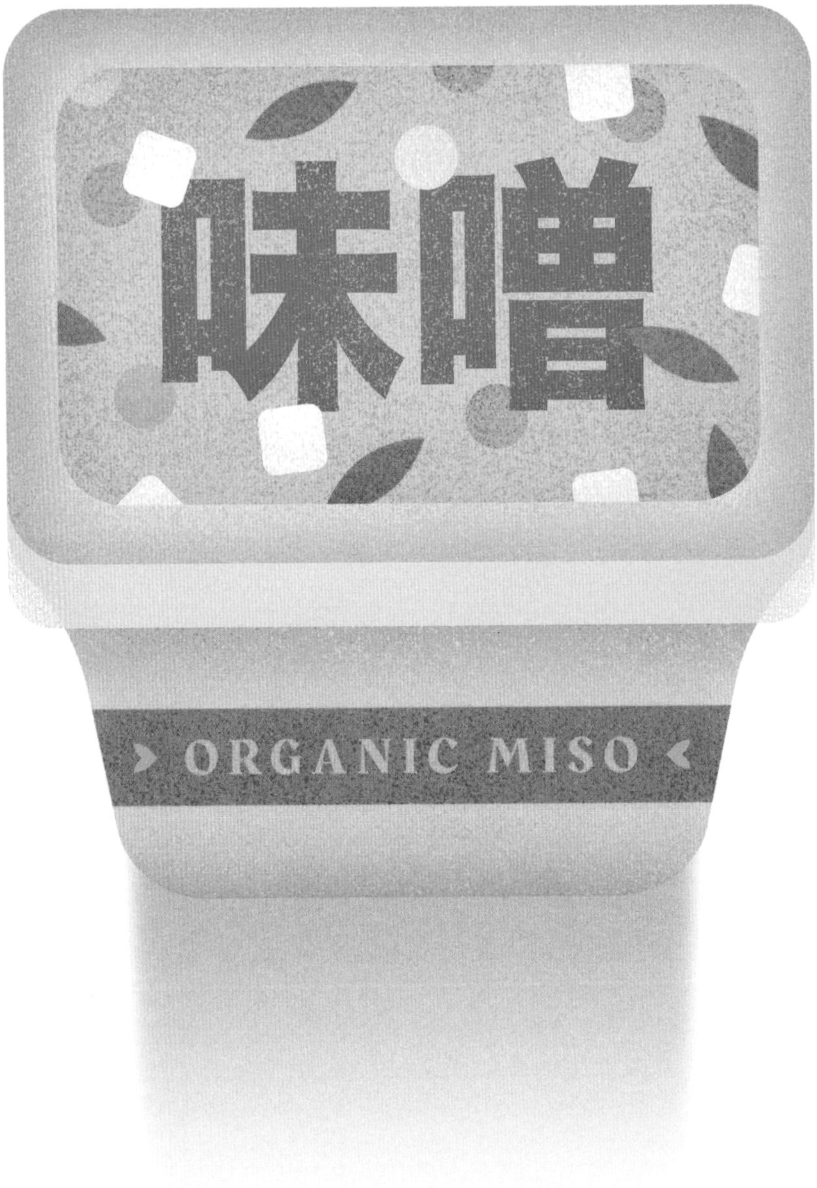
味噌
ORGANIC MISO

Miso

This fermented paste, made from soy beans, rice or barley, koji (inoculated cooked rice), water, and salt, is your shortcut to umami (the fifth, savory taste, that's also found in mushrooms). Originating from Japan, a spoonful of miso offers so much opportunity, giving marinades for fish, meat, vegetables, dressings, stews, soups, and even desserts a serious flavor boost. Of course, not all miso is equal; it can vary in both color and potency. White (or shiro), for example, is creamy, sweet, and the least salty, making it the most versatile and a good place to start for the uninitiated.

VARIETIES	The color of your miso will, in general, indicate how intense and salty it will taste—the darker it is, the stronger and saltier it will be.
PAIR WITH	Veg (alliums, roots, eggplant, green beans, tomato), chicken wings, pork chops, crab, tofu, beans, egg, mustard, yogurt, honey, chocolate, and banana.
TRANSFORM	Just a tbsp. stirred into hot broth or dashi, with some cooked noodles and greens, is a welcome lunch or dinner.

Miso, asparagus, and pea risotto

2 tbsp. white miso
1 large onion, diced
2 garlic cloves, sliced
Glug of olive oil
¾ cup arborio rice
⅜ cup white wine
1½ cups sliced asparagus
Handful frozen peas
Half a lemon, zested
Grated Parmesan,
 to serve

This simple miso broth brings a richness and complexity to this wholly untraditional risotto, without overpowering.

First, get your broth ready: whisk the white miso into 4 cups water in a saucepan on the back of the stovetop, and bring to a simmer. Meanwhile, in another pan saute the onion and garlic in a good glug of olive oil, until the onion is soft and translucent. Add the arborio rice, stirring until every grain glistens. Add the white wine, stirring until it has been absorbed. Now, start adding the miso broth a ladleful at a time, stirring and allowing it to be absorbed before adding the next. Keep going until the rice is cooked and plump.

Meanwhile, heat some oil in another pan and add the sliced asparagus. Cook until tender, adding the frozen peas in the last few minutes of cooking. Add the lemon zest, season well, and set aside. Once the rice is cooked, stir in the vegetables and serve with grated Parmesan. Serves 2.

Chocolate, miso, and pecan cookies

½ cup + 3 tbsp. butter,
 softened
1 cup brown sugar (packed)
1 egg
3 tbsp. white miso
2 cups all-purpose flour
1 tsp. baking powder
¾ tsp. baking soda
⅔ cup dark chocolate,
 chopped
¾ cup pecans

Stash a few of these salty-sweet cookies in the freezer for emergency moments. Do swap the pecans for walnuts, if that's your preference.

Cream together the butter and sugar, then whisk in the egg followed by the miso. Sift together the all-purpose flour, baking powder, and baking soda, then mix into the butter. Add the chopped dark chocolate and pecans, combine, then refrigerate for 30 minutes.

Preheat the oven to 350°F. Scoop out tablespoons of the mixture onto a lined cookie sheet and bake for 14–16 minutes, until firm to the touch. Leave to cool on the sheet for a few minutes before transferring to a wire rack to cool completely. Makes 12–16.

Miso deviled eggs

3 eggs
2½ tsp. mayonnaise
½ tsp. Dijon mustard
1½ tsp. white miso
Dash of rice vinegar
Handful chopped chives
Sprinkling of sesame seeds

Deviled eggs never fail to get a party started. Get ahead by boiling the eggs the day before and storing in the refrigerator, ready to assemble before your guests arrive.

Boil the eggs for 11 minutes, then drain and rinse under cold water. Once cool enough to handle, peel then slice in half lengthwise. Scoop out the yolks and mash in a bowl with a fork. Mix in the mayonnaise, mustard, white miso, rice vinegar, and chopped chives. Taste and adjust accordingly. Spoon into the hollowed-out eggs and garnish with more chopped chives and some sesame seeds. Makes 6.

Red miso and shiitake ramen

1 tsp. sesame oil
Thumb-size piece of
    ginger, minced
1 red chile, finely chopped
2 tbsp. red miso
2 cups broth
2 cups shiitake mushrooms,
    finely chopped
1¼ cups bok choi leaves
1 tsp. soy sauce
3 scallions, sliced
2 nests egg noodles, cooked

To make more of a meal of this spicy soup, top with halved boiled eggs or pork belly.

Heat the sesame oil in a large saucepan, add the ginger and red chile. Fry for 1 minute until fragrant, then stir in the red miso and the broth. Bring to a simmer, stirring until the miso has dissolved, then add the shiitake and bok choi. Simmer for 5 minutes, then add the soy sauce and scallions. Take two deep bowls, put a nest of cooked egg noodles in each, and divide the broth equally. Serves 2.

Miso eggplant fries

2 tbsp. brown miso paste
1½ tbsp. golden honey
1 tbsp. soy sauce
1 tbsp. mirin
1 tsp. sesame oil
Pinch of red pepper flakes
1 large eggplant
Small handful
    sesame seeds
Scallions, chopped, to serve

The beauty of eggplants is they are very receptive to any flavor you throw at them, which in this case is miso.

Preheat the oven to 400°F. In a small bowl, whisk together the brown miso, honey, soy sauce, mirin, sesame oil, and red pepper flakes. Cut the eggplant into wedges, toss in the marinade to coat, and transfer to a baking sheet lined with parchment paper. Scatter with sesame seeds and bake for 20 minutes, turning halfway through cooking and brushing with more marinade and sprinkling with more sesame seeds, until the eggplant is golden brown. Serve with a scattering of chopped scallions. Serves 2, as a side.

Tahini

Synonymous with Middle Eastern, North African, and Mediterranean cooking, this nutty, creamy paste is one of the most reached-for in my pantry. Made from hulled (generally white) sesame kernels, which are then roasted and crushed, the resulting sweet-savory paste works a dream with roast vegetables, grilled meat, fish, as a dressing, in hummus, of course... the list goes on. Tahini rubs along well with candies, too: drizzle into brownies or blondies, cake batters, cookies, buns, truffles, or even mugs of hot chocolate. Usually sold in a jar, be sure to give it a good stir to blend the oil and pulp before using.

PAIR WITH	Dates, pomegranate, vanilla, yogurt, vegetables (cauliflower, eggplant, squash, sprouts), eggs, chickpeas, spices (such as cinnamon), chicken, mackerel, halibut, lentils, and chocolate.
TRANSFORM	Spread on toast with a little golden honey and some crushed walnuts for an easy breakfast or stir into soups for an instant flavor boost.
HACK	While you can store it in the refrigerator, the cold makes tahini thicken. Instead, keep sealed in a cool, dark place away from heat.

Zucchini, mint, and tahini soup

Olive oil
1 onion, finely diced
3 garlic cloves, chopped
4 zucchini, sliced into half
   moons
3 cups vegetable broth
Handful mint leaves
1 lemon, juiced
2 tbsp. tahini

A simple soup to serve warm or refrigerated, with crusty bread to mop it all up.

Heat a good glug of oil in a saucepan and cook the onion until softened, about 10 minutes. Add the garlic, stir for 1 minute, then add the zucchini. Cook, stirring occasionally, until slightly softened, then add the broth and season. Bring to a boil, cover, and simmer for 15 minutes.

Blitz using an immersion blender, then add a big handful of mint leaves and blitz again. Stir in the lemon juice and tahini. Serve drizzled with more tahini and some chopped mint if you like. Serves 4.

Tahini, date, and cinnamon porridge

½ cup rolled oats
2 cups milk
3 dates, pitted and sliced
1 tsp. cinnamon
2 tsp. tahini
Sesame seeds

Top with extra chopped dates or fresh fruit, such as sliced banana.

Put the oats, milk (cow, oat, or nut), dates, and cinnamon in a saucepan. Cook over medium heat, stirring, until thick and creamy—about 5 minutes. Stir through the tahini and serve scatted with sesame seeds. Serves 1.

Tahini butter

¼ cup unsalted butter,
   softened
1½ tbsp. tahini
1 tbsp. soy sauce
½ tbsp. lemon juice
½ tsp. maple syrup

Toss this through roast vegetables, chickpeas, or grains to add an irresistible richness.

In a bowl, combine the butter, tahini, soy sauce, lemon juice, and maple syrup—this will take a few minutes, so keep mixing. Taste and adjust if needed. Serves 4.

Whipped tahini with squash and pine nuts

1 butternut squash
1 red onion
2 tbsp. olive oil
2½ tbsp. pine nuts
½ cup tahini
Half a lemon, juiced
Za'atar, to serve
Handful parsley, chopped

The whipped tahini is the star here, adding a rich, nutty base for the sweet roast squash.

Preheat the oven to 400°F. Peel and cut the butternut squash and onion into wedges, then transfer to an ovenproof dish. Toss with the olive oil and some salt and pepper, and roast, stirring occasionally, for 45 minutes to 1 hour, until the vegetables are cooked through. Set aside to cool.

Meanwhile, add a little oil to a sacuepan over medium heat and toast the pine nuts with a pinch of salt, turning occasionally, for a couple of minutes, until golden. Transfer to a bowl.

In another bowl, whisk the tahini with ⅜ cup water and a pinch of salt. Add the lemon juice and taste. Spread the whipped tahini on a plate, top with the squash and onions, then scatter over the pine nuts, some za'atar, and the parsley. Serves 4, as a side.

Tahini and chocolate banana bread

2 ripe bananas
2 tbsp. tahini
½ cup + 3 tbsp. unsalted butter, softened
⅔ cup light brown sugar, packed
4 tbsp. golden honey
2 eggs
1⅔ cups all-purpose flour
1 tsp. baking powder
1 tsp. ground cardamom seeds
¾ cup dark chocolate, chopped

A not-too-sweet, spiced banana bread studded with dark chocolate that can be eaten as it is or sliced and popped under the grill.

Preheat the oven to 350°F. In a bowl, mash the bananas with tahini until combined. In a separate bowl, use an electric mixer to whisk the butter, superfine sugar, and honey, until pale and soft. Gradually beat in the eggs, whisking between each addition, until combined. Add the banana mix and stir well.

Fold in the flour, baking powder, cardamom, and chopped dark chocolate. Pour into a greased and lined 1lb. loaf pan and smooth the top. Bake for 1 hour to 1 hour and 10 minutes until a toothpick inserted into the center comes out clean, covering with aluminum foil if the top browns too quickly. Leave to cool completely in the pan before removing and slicing. Serves 10.

Canned tomatoes

Chopped, plum, cherry... canned tomatoes are dinner insurance, and the gateway to pasta sauces, curries, shakshuka, soups, and stews. In short, they are a cook's comfort blanket. Canned tomatoes are often better than their fresh counterpart (depending on where you live, of course); picked at peak ripeness and preserved to maintain that sweet, slightly acidic flavor all year round, especially when fresh tomatoes are of questionable quality. While there's often lots of choice, the better quality your tomatoes, the more flavorful your meals will be. Whole plum tomatoes tend to be the best bet for a good flesh-to-juice ratio, and you can easily break them up if needed.

VARIETIES	With their chunky texture, chopped tomatoes are perfect for long-simmering casseroles, soups, and curries. Sweet cherry tomatoes are ideal for quick sauces; fleshier plum tomatoes are more versatile and can be used for both long and short cooking (and you can chop, crush, or leave them whole).
TRANSFORM	A simple, yet satisfying, sauce can be achieved by frying a chopped onion in olive oil until soft, stirring in garlic, followed by a can of plum tomatoes, breaking them up with a wooden spoon. Add sugar and red wine vinegar to taste, simmer until thick, and finish with torn basil leaves.
HACK	Rinse empty tomato cans with a little water and add to your recipe—it will ensure you get every last bit and, once reduced, will add more flavor.

Tomato chana dal

2 tsp. coconut oil
2 shallots, sliced
Thumb-size piece
  of ginger, minced
1 red chile, sliced
2 garlic cloves, sliced
1 tsp. mustard seeds
1½ tsp. ground cumin
½ tsp. garam masala
1 can (13½ fl. oz.) coconut
  milk
1 can (14½ oz.) chopped
  tomatoes
2½ cups cooked chana dal

**For a nice bit of texture, serve topped with a handful
of cooked chana dal roasted with salt and chile.**

Heat the coconut oil in a large saucepan, add the shallots, ginger,
red chile, and garlic, and fry, stirring occasionally, for 10 minutes.
Add the mustard seeds, ground cumin, and garam masala, and
cook for a couple of minutes until fragrant. Add the coconut milk,
tomatoes, and half a can's worth of water, and simmer for 10
minutes. Add the cooked chana dal to the pan and continue cooking
for 5 minutes, until heated through. Serve topped with cilantro,
natural yogurt, and some naan bread on the side. Serves 4.

Baked gnocchi with sausage and kale

16-ounce package gnocchi
Glug of olive oil
4 sausages
Good pinch of red pepper
  flakes
1 tsp. fennel seeds
1½ cups chopped kale
1 can (14½ oz.) chopped
  tomatoes
1½ tbsp. grated Parmesan

**A throw-it-all-together pan bake for when you're short on time
and inclination.**

Preheat the oven to 400°F. Put the gnocchi in a bowl, cover with
boiling water, leave to stand for 2 minutes, then drain.
    Heat a glug of olive oil in a large ovenproof pan. Cut open the
sausages and squeeze the meat from the skins into the pan. Add
the red pepper flakes and fennel seeds and fry, stirring occasionally,
until the sausages are cooked through and golden, about 8 minutes.
Add the kale in the last few minutes of cooking. Tip in the chopped
tomatoes, season, then bring to a simmer. Add the drained gnocchi,
stir, then turn off the heat and scatter with the grated Parmesan.
Bake for 15 minutes. Serves 2.

Fasolakia (Greek green beans)

2 tbsp. olive oil
1 onion, finely diced
4 garlic cloves, crushed
1 tsp. dried oregano
4 cups green beans
1 can (14½ oz.) chopped
  tomatoes
1 lemon, juiced
Handful dill, chopped

**Green beans slow cooked in tomatoes until tender, ready to be
eaten (hot or cold) with meat or as part of a vegetarian spread.**

Heat the olive oil in a large saucepan. Add the onion, garlic, and a
pinch of salt, and cook until softened. Add the oregano, topped and
tailed green beans, chopped tomatoes, and 1 cup water, and simmer
for 40 minutes. Season, add lemon juice to taste and a handful of
chopped dill. Serves 4 as a side.

Baked eggs with avocado

Glug of olive oil
1 onion, diced
1 red bell pepper, diced
2 garlic cloves, crushed
1 tsp. paprika
Red pepper flakes, to taste
1 can (14½ oz.) chopped
   tomatoes
4 eggs
2 avocados
1 lime, juiced
Cilantro leaves

Baked eggs are a no-brainer any time of day, but this makes an especially good brunch with toast or flatbread on the side.

Heat a glug of oil in a saucepan over medium heat, then cook the onion until soft, about 10 minutes. Add the red pepper, garlic, paprika, and red pepper flakes, and cook for a few minutes. Add the chopped tomatoes, season, and simmer, about 12 minutes, until reduced and thickened. Make gaps in the sauce, crack in the eggs, cover, and cook for 5 or 6 minutes, or until the whites are set.

In a bowl, mash the avocados with the lime juice and some salt and pepper. Once the eggs are cooked, top with the avocado, garnish with cilantro leaves, and serve. Serves 2.

Tomato and feta orzo

1 tbsp. olive oil
1 red onion, chopped
2 garlic cloves, crushed
Pinch of red pepper flakes
1 tbsp. tomato paste
1 can (14½ oz.) chopped
   tomatoes
2 cups broth
1 bay leaf
2 cups orzo
⅔ cup feta, crumbled
Squeeze of lemon juice
Handful parsley, chopped

Keep this simple, or top with green olive gremolata made by combining 4 tablespoons chopped green olives, 1 teaspoon lemon zest, a squeeze of lemon juice, 1 tablespoon olive oil, 1 small, crushed garlic clove, and 1 small bunch chopped parsley.

Preheat the oven to 425°F. Meanwhile heat the olive oil in an ovenproof saucepan over medium heat. Add the red onion and cook, stirring, until softened, about 10 minutes. Add the garlic and red pepper flakes, and cook for another minute. Add the tomato paste, chopped tomatoes, broth, bay leaf, orzo, and a generous grind of black pepper. Bring to a simmer, cover, and transfer to the preheated oven for 20 minutes, until the orzo is cooked. Stir in the crumbled feta, lemon juice, and chopped parsley. Serves 3-4.

Butter beans

These large, creamy beans are so dependable and skew the effort-to-reward ratio in favor of the reward. Their soft, floury texture means they play well with meat (pork, chicken, duck), fish (white fish, mackerel, tuna), vegetables (squash, peppers, leek, carrot, zucchini) and in myriad dishes, from soups, salads, and dips, to stews and pies, or if you're feeling lazy, a meal in their own right. While canned or jarred butter beans are the path to easy meals, there are advantages to the dried kind, too. You do need to remember to soak them overnight, but the bonus is that you'll have more control over their cooking (canned and jarred are cooked and therefore soft), and they'll soak up the flavor of whatever they encounter.

TRANSFORM	Swap pasta for beans, tossing in your favorite sauce, from puttanesca to pesto, for a speedy meal.
HEALTH	A good source of fiber, protein, complex carbs, and minerals (such as potassium and magnesium).
HACK	For the creamiest butter bean mash, blend with a tablespoon or two of the starchy can liquid.

Cacio e pepe butter beans

1 tbsp. olive oil
1 garlic clove, crushed
1 can (15½ oz.) butter beans, drained
4 tbsp. grated Parmesan, plus the rind
2 tbsp. butter
Black pepper

Roman cacio e pepe (which translates to "cheese and pepper") is beautiful in its simplicity and quick to pull together. Traditionally served with pasta, the sauce works equally well with butter beans. Just add greens and a pork chop.

Heat the oil in a saucepan, add the garlic and cook, stirring, for a minute. Add the drained butter beans, Parmesan rind, and ⅜ cup water, and bring to a simmer. Once the beans are warmed through, take off the heat, remove the rind, and fold through the butter. Add a very generous amount of black pepper (about 40 grinds) and the grated Parmesan, stirring so everything emulsifies, and serve immediately. Serves 2.

Spiced shepherd's pie with butter bean mash

Glug of olive oil
2 shallots, finely chopped
1 cup ground beef
2 garlic cloves, crushed
1 tsp. ground cumin
1 tsp. ground cinnamon
1 tbsp. tomato paste
2 tbsp. rose harissa
1 cup broth
⅔ cup frozen peas
1 jar (24¾ oz.) butter beans, drained and rinsed
1 tbsp. tahini

Mashed potato is swapped for butter beans, tahini, and olive oil to create something altogether lighter.

Heat a good glug of oil in a saucepan, add the shallots, and cook until softened. Add the ground beef, breaking up the meat with the back of a spoon and frying until crisp, about 5 minutes. Add the garlic, ground cumin, ground cinnamon, tomato paste, rose harissa, and a pinch of salt. Cook for a few minutes, then add the broth and frozen peas. Simmer, covered, for 30 minutes. Tip the mixture into an ovenproof dish and leave to cool a little.
    Preheat the oven to 375°F. Meanwhile, mash the butter beans in a bowl. Stir through the tahini, a drizzle of olive oil, and some seasoning. Spoon the mash over the mince and bake for 40 minutes until bubbling. Serves 2-3.

Pea and butter bean dip

1½ cups cooked frozen peas
1 cup butter beans, drained and rinsed
1 garlic clove, minced
1 scallion, chopped
2 tbsp. tahini
1 tbsp. olive oil
Squeeze of lemon juice

Butter beans mean a creamy texture, making this hummus perfect for spreading on toast or dipping crudites in.

Add the cooked frozen peas, butter beans, garlic, scallion, tahini, olive oil, lemon juice, and some seasoning to a food processor and blitz to a rough paste. With the motor still running, add 1 tablespoon water, and blitz again. Serves 4.

Marinated butter beans

2 tbsp. olive oil

2½ tbsp. white wine vinegar

1 shallot, diced

Half a lemon, zest and juice

1 jar (24¾ oz.) butter beans, drained and rinsed

Small handful parsley, chopped

This is one of those recipes that gets better with age, so make a batch up to three days in advance and use to pep up salads.

In a small bowl, whisk together the olive oil, white wine vinegar, shallot, lemon zest and juice, and some salt and black pepper. Add the butter beans and the chopped parsley, and combine again. Taste and adjust the seasoning if need be. Leave to marinate for at least 15 minutes. Store, covered, in the refrigerator for up to three days. Serves 4-6.

Harissa and fennel butter beans with herby yogurt

Olive oil

1 red onion, sliced

1 garlic clove, sliced

1 fennel bulb, finely chopeed

1 lemon, zested and juiced

1 tbsp. rose harissa

Handful mint, chopped

1 jar (14 oz.) butter beans, drained

¾ cup plain yogurt

A hunk of crusty bread is the vehicle of choice for scooping up these sticky, spicy beans.

Heat 1 tablespoon olive oil in a skillet and, once hot, fry the red onion and garlic with a pinch of salt for 2 minutes. Add the fennel and cook until softened, about 10 minutes. Add the lemon zest and the harissa and cook, stirring, for a minute. Add the chopped mint (keeping a little back) and the butter beans, and warm through.

Meanwhile, in a small bowl whisk together the yogurt, lemon juice, a drizzle of olive oil, a good pinch of salt, and the reserved mint. Adjust the seasoning if necessary. Spoon the beans into bowls and top with the herby yogurt. Serves 2.

Canned pineapple

Canned pineapple has something of a dubious reputation, renowned for bringing the retro fun to cheese-and-pineapple hedgehogs, fruit cups, and pizza, alongside ham. There is, however, more to the canned tropical fruit than a heavy dose of nostalgia. Available in perfectly even rings and chunks, its sweet-and-sour ways stand up well to baking, be it in a crumble or cake (an upside-down or carrot cake being classics) and savory dishes such as curries and fried rice.

PAIRS WITH	Chicken, turkey, pork, shrimp, coconut, chile, ginger, butternut squash, sweet potato, banana, cherry, lime, rice, caramel, and rum.
HEALTH	A source of vitamin C, fiber, and potassium, and a half-cup portion counts toward your five-a-day. Be sure to go for cans with no added sugar.
HACK	Don't ditch the can juices. Instead, heat sugar and water, add the pineapple juice along with lime juice, then freeze in a container for granita, sunny side up.

Pineapple and ginger upside-down cake

Everyone knows the best part of this nostalgic cake is the sticky, caramelized pineapple. Here, stem ginger brings extra stickiness, while using a splash of the fruit juice in the sponge adds flavor.

FOR THE TOPPING

2 tbsp. light brown sugar

2 tbsp. unsalted butter, softened, plus extra for greasing

5 canned pineapple rings

FOR THE CAKE

¾ cup + 2 tbsp. unsalted butter, softened

¾ cup + 2 tbsp. light brown sugar, packed

3 eggs

1 tsp. vanilla bean paste

2 cups + 1½ tbsp. self-rising flour

½ tsp. baking powder

3 balls of stem ginger in syrup, chopped

Preheat the oven to 375°F and grease and line an 8-inch round cake pan. For the topping, mix the light brown sugar with the butter, then spread on the base of the pan. Drain and pat dry five canned pineapple rings, reserving the liquid. Place a whole ring in the middle of the pan, then halve the remaining rings and arrange in the pan.

For the cake, cream the butter and light brown sugar together. Add the eggs, mixing well between each addition, then add the vanilla bean paste. Sift in the self-rising flour, baking powder, and a pinch of salt. Add 2 tablespoons of the reserved pineapple juice and the stem ginger. Pour the batter over the pineapple rings and level. Bake for 50 minutes, until a toothpick inserted into the center comes out clean, covering with aluminum foil if the top browns too much. Leave to cool for a few minutes, then run a knife around the edge to loosen, and turn out onto a board. Brush with the stem ginger syrup and serve warm. Serves 12.

Pineapple and green bean curry

A simple, comforting curry that would welcome chicken, shrimp, or tofu.

1 tsp. coconut oil

3 shallots, finely sliced

2 garlic cloves, finely chopped

Thumb-size piece of ginger, minced

1 tsp. cilantro seeds, crushed

1 tbsp. red curry paste

1 cup coconut milk

1 cup broth

1¾ cups green beans, topped, tailed, and halved

1 cup canned pineapple chunks, drained

Handful cilantro leaves

Heat the coconut oil in a saucepan over medium heat and fry the shallots for 4 minutes. Add the garlic and ginger, and continue to cook for a minute. Add the cilantro seeds, cook for another minute until fragrant, then add the red curry paste, coconut milk, and broth, and bring to a simmer. Add the green beans and cook until tender, about 5 minutes. Stir in the canned pineapple chunks and cook for a few minutes more, just to warm through. Serve with cilantro leaves and rice. Serves 2 as a main or 4 as part of a spread.

Mini carrot and pineapple cakes

While these cakes don't need it, you could top them with a layer of soft cheese frosting.

¼ cup + 1 tbsp. light brown sugar, packed
¼ cup + 1 tsp. self-rising whole-wheat flour
½ tsp. baking soda
1 tsp. ground cinnamon
Pinch of nutmeg
Half an orange, zested
1 egg
¼ cup + 1 tbsp. sunflower oil
1 cup grated carrot
⅓ cup broken-up walnuts
⅓ cup canned pineapple chunks, chopped

Preheat the oven to 350°F and line six holes of a muffin pan with paper baking cups. In a large bowl, mix the brown sugar, flour, baking soda, ground cinnamon, nutmeg, and the orange zest. In a separate bowl, whisk together the egg and sunflower oil, then stir into the flour mix with the grated carrot, walnuts, canned pineapple chunks, and a pinch of salt. Divide the mixture between the paper baking cups and bake for 20-23 minutes, until a toothpick inserted into the center comes out clean. Leave on a wire rack to cool. Makes 6.

Fried pineapple rice

Successful crispy rice hinges on day-old, refrigerator-cold rice. If, however, you're starting from scratch, be sure to let the rice cool completely. Eat with garlic shrimp or greens, such as bok choi.

1 cup cooked jasmine rice
2 tbsp. soy sauce
Drizzle of sesame oil
Drizzle of peanut oil
1 garlic clove, crushed
1 egg
Half a red bell pepper, chopped
Half a green bell pepper, chopped
⅔ cup canned pineapple chunks
¼ cup cashews
Scallions, sliced, to serve

Put the cold, cooked jasmine rice in a bowl, add the soy sauce and sesame oil, and combine. Add the peanut oil to a wok, fry the garlic for a minute, then add to the rice bowl. Add a little more oil to the wok, crack in an egg and stir quickly to scramble, then add to the bowl. Fry the bell peppers until softened, then add the pineapple chunks and cashews, and fry again until hot. Tip the lot into the bowl and give everything a good mix. Add a little more oil to the wok, tip in the rice mix, pat down with a spoon, and cook for 8-10 minutes until the bottom is crisp. Flip onto a plate and serve sprinkled with sliced scallions. Serves 6.

Bacon and pineapple hash

Pork and pineapple are a combination you either love or hate. If you're in the former camp, this spiced potato hash is for you.

10½ oz. Yukon Gold potatoes
Drizzle of oil
3 slices of bacon, cut into pieces
2 sprigs thyme
¼ tsp. allspice
Pinch of cayenne pepper
3/4 cup canned pineapple chunks
4 eggs
Cilantro, chopped, to serve
Red chile, sliced, to serve

Chop the potatoes into chunks, then boil in salted water until tender, about 8 minutes. Drain and steam dry. Heat the oil in a skillet, then fry the bacon until crispy. Add the potato chunks, the leaves from the thyme, allspice, and cayenne, and continue to fry, stirring occasionally, for 10 minutes. Add the canned pineapple chunks, warm through for a couple of minutes, then season. Make four gaps in the potato mix, crack in the eggs, cover, and cook until the whites are set and the yolks runny, about 6 minutes. Serve with cilantro and red chile scattered over. Serves 2.

Artichokes

Artichokes can be a challenge. Technically a thistle, these round things require a fair bit of preparation before the leaves can be picked and dipped in butter, or the fleshy heart reached and shaved into a salad. Artichoke hearts preserved in oil, meanwhile, take away all the chopping and trimming, which not only saves on time, but this approach also means you can be liberal with how many you use to spark up pizzas and crostini, risottos, or omelets, roast in pan bakes, or simply eat from the jar with a cocktail in hand. And, bonus: you can do this all year around.

PAIRS WITH	Chicken, steak, salmon, white fish, eggs, Parmesan, feta, ricotta, mozzarella, spinach, kale, potato, tomato, yogurt, pasta, and rice.
TRANSFORM	Up the flavor ante by roasting marinated artichoke hearts (drizzle with a little oil) until browned. Then add to salads or serve with aioli as a snack.
HACK	Don't throw away the liquid. As this is made up of things like oil, vinegar, and salt, it's ideal for dressing salads or vegetables. Bring it to life by adding some more olive oil, maybe mustard, garlic, shallot, and some herbs.

Artichoke and lemon pasta

7 oz. spaghetti
1 lemon, zested
   and juiced
2 tbsp. olive oil
½ cup Parmesan, grated
3½ oz. jarred artichoke
   hearts, sliced
Handful basil, torn

**Everyone needs a lemony pasta in their repertoire, and this
one couldn't be easier.**

Cook the spaghetti in a saucepan of boiling salted water according
to the package instructions. Meanwhile, in a large bowl combine the
lemon zest and juice, olive oil, and Parmesan. Season generously
with black pepper, then stir in the artichokes. Scoop the spaghetti
from the pan into the bowl, then toss, adding some pasta cooking
water to loosen. Stir in the basil and serve with more grated
Parmesan. Serves 2.

Spinach and artichoke dip

7 oz. jarred artichoke
   hearts, drained
Handful baby spinach
¼ cup pine nuts, toasted
Half a lemon
2 tbsp. Parmesan, grated
Handful basil leaves
3 tbsp. olive oil

**Chuck everything into a food processor, whizz, and you're good to
go. Just add breadsticks and crudites.**

Put the artichokes in a food processor along with the rest of the
ingredients. Season and blitz smooth. Serves 4-6.

Artichoke skillet pie

Olive oil
1 small onion, chopped
2 leeks, chopped
1 garlic clove, crushed
7 oz. jarred artichoke hearts,
   drained and roughly
   chopped
7 oz. phyllo dugh
¾ cup ricotta
1 egg
Small handful tarragon,
   chopped
Small handful chives,
   chopped

**Heating the pie on the stovetop for a few minutes before
transferring to the oven ensures a crisp bottom. Turn the pan
halfway through cooking to ensure the pastry cooks evenly.**

Heat a little oil in an ovenproof skillet, then cook the onion and
leeks until softened. Add the garlic, cook until fragrant, then stir
through the artichokes and some seasoning. Set aside in a bowl.
   Preheat the oven to 425°F. Put a layer of phyllo dough over
the skillet, leaving a little overlap around the edges. Drizzle with oil,
then keep layering the pastry (drizzling oil between each layer) until
it's sturdy—about four layers. Drizzle the final layer with a little oil
and use a brush to spread it all over. In a bowl, combine the ricotta,
egg, the herbs, and some black pepper. Stir in the artichoke mix and
tip onto the dough. Cook over medium heat for a few minutes, then
fold the excess dough over the filling. Brush with a little more oil,
then bake for 20-25 minutes, until golden and crisp. Serves 6.

Artichoke panzanella

4 slices stale, crusty bread
2–3 tbsp. olive oil
1 red onion, finely sliced
Half a lemon, juiced
6 jarred artichoke hearts, finely sliced
20 tomatoes of varying sizes, cut into chunks
Large handful basil, torn
Large handful mint, torn

You have lots of options when it comes to panzanella, so be as inventive as you like.

Tear the bread into pieces and put in a roasting pan. Massage with olive oil and bake in a low oven until golden. Meanwhile, put the onion in a small bowl with a pinch of salt and set aside for 10 minutes (this will remove any bitterness).

In a large bowl, whisk 2 tablespoons olive oil, the lemon juice, and a pinch of salt. Add the artichokes, tomatoes, onion, and herbs. Season with black pepper, then add the bread. Give everything a good stir, then leave for 15 minutes before eating. Serves 4.

Artichoke, pea, and spelt salad

¾ cup frozen peas
½ cup spelt
1 tsp. white wine vinegar
1 tsp. Dijon mustard
Drizzle of olive oil
Lemon
Handful mint, chopped
7 oz. jarred artichoke hearts, sliced
1 romaine lettuce, torn

Spelt has a really good texture, making it ideal for salads. Cook a big batch to see you through the week.

Fill a medium saucepan with cold water and bring to a boil. Add the peas, cook for 1 minute, then remove with a slotted spoon and plunge into cold water. Drain the peas and set aside. Tip the spelt into a boiling water with a pinch of salt and cook until tender, 22–25 minutes. Drain and cool.

In a large bowl, whisk together the vinegar, mustard, a good drizzle of olive oil, a squeeze of lemon, and the mint. Season, then add the artichokes, lettuce, peas, and spelt. Give everything a good mix. Serves 4.

Cannellini beans

These Italian, kidney-shaped beans are something of a miracle ingredient. With a slightly nutty flavor and lovely, firm texture, a fistful will add body to soups and stews, bulk up salads, and, when blitzed with a just a few other ingredients, transform into a luscious, creamy dip. Not only do beans mean easy, budget-friendly meals, but they're good for us (being a source of fiber and protein, meaning we feel fuller for longer) and the planet to boot—they have a low water footprint compared with other protein sources.

COOK	Drain, rinse and they're ready to be mashed and spread on toast or blended into a dip; toss through salads; warm through stews and soups; braise with rosemary, onions, and tomatoes, or slow cook with sausages. If, however, you have more time, try the dry kind—yes, they require soaking (about eight hours) and cooking (one hour), but you'll get more flavor.
SWAP	In most cases, white beans can be used interchangeably. When you're out of cannellini, try great northern beans, navy, or if color doesn't matter, then adzuki.
HACK	These beans can help pull off creamy vegan pasta sauces; add a can to tomato sauce and blend, alternatively simply mash with some pasta cooking water then liven up with olive oil, lemon zest, and herbs.

FAGIOLI
CANNELLINI

BIOLOGICI

Chicken, leek, and bean pan bake

1 tbsp. olive oil
2 bone-in chicken thighs
2 leeks, sliced into rounds
1 garlic clove, crushed
⅜ cup white wine
Half a lemon, zested
1 cup broth
1¼ cups canned cannellini
  beans, drained and
  rinsed

The key to success here is to get some good color on the chicken thighs before adding the leeks.

Preheat the oven to 400°F. Warm the olive oil in a large ovenproof casserole dish. Season the chicken thighs and cook skin-side down until golden and crisp, about 5 minutes. Remove the chicken from the pan and set aside. Add the leeks and the garlic and cook for 5 minutes, until softened. Pour in the white wine, allow to bubble for a couple of minutes, then add the lemon zest, broth, and the cannellini beans. Turn off the heat, nestle the chicken back in the pan, and season. Cook in the preheated oven for 35-40 minutes, until the chicken is cooked through. Serves 1, generously.

Pasta e fagioli

Glug of olive oil
1 onion, finely chopped
1 celery stalk, finely chopped
1 large carrot, finely chopped
1 garlic clove, crushed
1 sprig rosemary, leaves
  finely chopped
Pinch of red pepper flakes
4 cups vegetable broth
1 can (14½ oz.) chopped
  tomatoes
1 can (15½ oz.) cannellini
  beans, drained and rinsed
6 oz. small pasta shapes
  (e.g. ditalini)
2⅓ cups cavolo nero,
  roughly torn
Grated Parmesan

A generous, soupy dish of pasta and beans with as many versions as there are cooks. Don't be too prescriptive; mix up the herbs, use fresh tomatoes instead of canned in summer, and switch up the beans.

Heat a good glug of olive oil in a large saucepan and, once hot, add the onion, celery, and carrot. Cook for 10 minutes until lightly golden. Add the garlic, rosemary, and red pepper flakes and fry for about a minute longer. Add the vegetable broth and the chopped tomatoes and bring to a simmer. Add the cannellini beans, bring back to a simmer, and cook for 5 minutes. Using an immersion blender, pulse a couple of times to break up the beans (or use a masher), then add the pasta and cavolo nero, and cook, stirring occasionally so nothing sticks to the bottom, until the pasta is cooked. Season to taste, ladle into bowls, and serve with grated Parmesan. Serves 4.

Garlicky cannellini mash

Glug of olive oil
1 shallot, finely chopped
3 garlic cloves, crushed
2 sprigs thyme
1 can (15½ oz.) cannellini
  beans, drained and rinsed
⅜ cup broth
Squeeze of lemon juice

Delicious with sausages, steak, or white fish.

Heat a little olive oil in a skillet, then add the shallot, garlic, and the leaves from the thyme, and cook until fragrant. Add the cannellini beans and broth (vegetable or chicken), bring to a boil, then reduce the heat and simmer for 10 minutes. Mash with a potato masher or fork, then add the lemon juice, a good grind of black pepper, and a drizzle of olive oil. Serves 2.

Greens and bean crumble

The humble crumble gets a savory makeover. This comforting bake requires no more than a side salad, although it also pairs well with a roast.

FOR THE TOPPING

2 tbsp. unsalted butter, cubed

⅔ cup rolled oats

⅓ cup all-purpose flour

2 tbsp. hazelnuts, toasted and chopped

1 tbsp. pumpkin seeds

FOR THE FILLING

1 large onion, chopped

1 tbsp. olive oil

1 garlic clove, minced

2¼ cups green cabbage, shredded

1 cup sour cream

1 tbsp. wholegrain mustard

1 cup vegetable broth

1 can (15½ oz.) cannellini beans, drained and rinsed

2 tsp. thyme leaves

Sprinkle of grated Parmesan

Make the topping by rubbing together the butter, oats, flour, hazelnuts, and pumpkin seeds. Set aside in the refrigerator. Fry the onion in the olive oil for 10 minutes, adding the garlic in the last minute. Add the shredded cabbage and cook for another 8–10 minutes until soft.

Preheat the oven to 400°F. In a bowl, combine the sour cream, wholegrain mustard, vegetable broth, cannellini beans, 1 teaspooon thyme leaves, and some seasoning. Combine with the vegetables, then tip into a baking dish and top with the crumble mix, remaining thyme leaves, and some grated Parmesan. Cook for 30 minutes, until the filling is bubbling. Serves 4

Cannellini and carrot burgers

Keep the uncooked burgers in the refrigerator for up to two days, or stash in the freezer for up to three months.

2 shallots, finely chopped

Glug of olive oil

3 cloves garlic, finely chopped

2¼ cups grated carrot

2 tsp. cumin seeds

1 can (15½ oz.) cannellini beans, drained and rinsed

2 tbsp. spelt flour

1 lemon, juiced

Cook the shallots in a glug of olive oil until golden. Add the garlic, grated carrot, cumin seeds, and some seasoning, and cook until the carrot has softened slightly, about 5 minutes.

In a bowl, mash the cannellini beans, then tip in the carrot mix, and combine with the spelt flour and the lemon juice. Taste and adjust the seasoning as needed. Shape into four patties and refrigerate for 30 minutes. Place on a lined baking sheet and bake in a preheated oven at 450°F for 20 minutes. Makes 4.

Canned sardines

Little fish—big flavor. A can of silvery sardines bathing in olive oil or tomato will give you a head start on your meal; already cooked, they're great in salads, piled on top of just-boiled rice or a slice of toast alongside tomatoes, onion, olive oil, and salt. When canned, all the worries of bones and freshness are eliminated, so all that's left to do is drain the oil and leave the sardines whole, flake, or mash them. And their strong, umami flavor means you don't need many to pack a punch—in sauces, dressings, tossed through pasta, or added to pan bakes in the last moments of cooking to crisp up. Caught at their best so all the goodness is preserved in their can, sardines are—if thoughtfully sourced—sustainable, too.

VARIETIES	When the sardines were caught, how they're prepared, and their size all impact your can. The number of fish your can houses indicates their size, varying from 3-4 up to 16-20. The larger the fish, the more tender and softer the flesh will be. Size aside, sardines can be canned with difference sauces, from olive oil and brine to tomato and chile.
HEALTH	These oily fish contain omega-3 fatty acids, protein, vitamin B12, and calcium, thanks to the soft bones that can be eaten.
HACK	Reserve the drained oil and use to cook vegetables in, or make dressings and condiments, such as mayonnaise.

Sardine, celery, and lemon salad

2 tbsp. olive oil
Half a lemon, zested and juiced
1 tsp. wholegrain mustard
Handful chives, chopped
Handful tarragon, chopped
1 tbsp. capers, drained and rinsed
3 celery stalks, diced
1 can (3¾ oz.) sardines, drained
A few lettuce leaves

Sardines and celery are a winning combination, but you could easily swap the lettuce for a cooked grain.

In a bowl, mix the olive oil, lemon zest and juice, wholegrain mustard, chives, tarragon, and capers. Add the celery, combine, then gently fold in the sardines. Season to taste, then add some lettuce leaves. Serves 2.

Sardine puttanesca and polenta

2 cans (3¾ oz. each) sardines
1 red onion, finely chopped
2 garlic cloves, finely sliced
Half a red chile, chopped
1 can (14½ oz.) chopped tomatoes
1 tbsp. tomato paste
¼ cup black olives, halved
1 tbsp. capers, drained and rinsed
2 cups broth (or water)
⅔ cup quick-cook polenta
1 tbsp. butter
Small handful fresh oregano

Anchovies are replaced with sardines in this hearty meal that makes good use of pantry ingredients.

Pour a little oil from one of the sardine cans into a saucepan, add the red onion and cook until softened, about 10 minutes. Add the garlic, red chile, chopped tomatoes, tomato paste, and ⅜ cup water. Season and simmer for 15 minutes, until thickened. Stir in the sardines, black olives, and capers, and cook for another 5 minutes.

Bring the broth (or water) to a boil, turn the heat down, and tip in the polenta, whisking constantly. Keep whisking for a few minutes until it is cooked—the mixture should come away from the side—then stir in the butter and some seasoning. Serve the puttanesca on top of the polenta and scatter with fresh oregano. Serves 2.

Fish cakes

9 oz. floury potatoes
4¼ oz. canned sardines
3 scallions, sliced
Large handful flat-leaf parsley, chopped
Half a lemon, zested and juiced
1 tbsp. all-purpose flour
1 egg, beaten
⅓ cup panko bread crumbs
2 tbsp. sunflower oil

Fish and potatoes are one of the great culinary love stories, and these budget-friendly fish cakes need little more than a crisp green salad and a wedge of lemon.

Cut the potatoes into chunks and simmer in boiling salted water until tender, about 10 minutes. Drain, leave to steam in the pan, then mash. Meanwhile, drain the sardines, put in a bowl, and mash with a fork. Add the scallions, parsley, lemon zest and juice, the mashed potato, season with pepper, and combine. With lightly floured hands, shape the mixture into four patties.

Dust the patties with flour, coat in beaten egg, then dip in the bread crumbs. To fry, heat the sunflower oil in a skillet and cook the fishcakes for about 3 minutes on each side until golden all over and cooked through. Serves 2.

Sardine Reuben

2 tsp. mayonnaise
½ tsp. horseradish sauce
1 tsp. tomato ketchup
Half a scallion, finely sliced
2 slices rye bread
2 canned sardines
2 slices Gruyère cheese
2 tbsp. sauerkraut
Small knob of butter
Cornichons, to serve

Canned sardines join the lineup of the best parts of the New York grilled sandwich—sharp, tangy sauerkraut, melting cheese, and a creamy dressing.

In a bowl, mix the mayonnaise, horseradish sauce, tomato ketchup, and scallion. Take the rye bread and spread with a layer of the dressing, then lay the sardines on top followed by the Gruyère and sauerkraut. Top with another slice of bread. Butter the outside of the sandwich and fry in a hot, nonstick pan until golden on both sides and the cheese has started to melt. Serve with cornichons. Serves 1.

Sardine linguine with pangrattato

2 tbsp. raisins
Glug of olive oil
⅓ cup pine nuts
½ cup dry bread crumbs
1 garlic clove, crushed
1 can (3¾ oz.) sardines, drained
2 shallots, finely sliced
1 tbsp. fennel seeds
7 oz. linguine
1 lemon, zested and juiced
A good pinch of saffron
Small handful parsley, chopped

A rustic, aromatic Sicilian pasta dish topped with crunchy bread crumbs.

First, soak the raisins in hot water. Then make the pangrattato: heat a little oil in a skillet, add the pine nuts, bread crumbs, and garlic. Fry, stirring occasionally, until crisp. Transfer to a small bowl.

Heat a splash of oil from the sardine can in the skillet, add the shallots and fennel seeds, and cook until golden and sticky. Drain the raisins, add them to the pan, along with some black pepper, and cook for a couple of minutes. Meanwhile, cook the linguine according to the package instructions.

Transfer the pasta to the onions, add a good splash of pasta cooking water, and toss to combine. Turn up the heat and stir in the drained sardines, lemon juice, saffron, and some seasoning. Simmer for 3 minutes, tossing until the pasta is well coated in the sauce—add more pasta water to loosen, if needed. Toss through some parsley and a little lemon zest, and serve sprinkled with the pangrattato. Serves 2.

Polenta

Hailing from northern Italy, polenta, or cornmeal, comes in many guises, and we should welcome them all—even the quick-cook stuff (although, admittedly, the consistency is harder to get right). From coarse to fine, yellow to white (which has a more delicate flavor), it is usually cooked by pouring it slowly through your fingers (a tip from Marcella Hazan) into a saucepan of boiling salted water (sometimes milk, or you could use broth) and whisking continuously. Let it thicken before turning down the heat and cooking for around 40 minutes. How often it needs stirring is, however, a point of contention, but every five minutes should do the trick. There are myriad things you can do with polenta, so it's always worth making more than you need.

PAIR WITH	Sausage, pancetta, chicken, seafood, mushroom, sweet corn, spinach, eggplant, cheese (Parmesan, feta, goat cheese), tomato, orange, blood orange, raspberry, apricot, rosemary and sage.
TRANSFORM	Polenta needs seasoning *very* generously to overcome its inherent blandness, so deploy generous amounts of olive oil or butter and Parmesan, and serve with something saucy.
HACK	Polenta sets when cold, so leftovers could be cut into triangles to be fried in oil and eaten with peperonata —or served with a negroni.

Baked polenta with tomatoes

2¾ cups cherry tomatoes
2 garlic cloves, sliced
1 tbsp. capers, drained
    and rinsed
Drizzle of olive oil
2 tbsp. fresh oregano,
    chopped
3¼ cups vegetable broth
¾ cup + 1 tbsp. polenta
½ cup Parmesan, grated

The polenta stays wonderfully creamy beneath its crisp, golden crust.

Preheat the oven to 325°F. Put the tomatoes, garlic, and capers on a baking sheet. Drizzle generously with oil, season with salt and pepper, and toss to coat. Roast for 45 minutes, stirring halfway through cooking. Once cool, stir through the oregano.

Turn the oven up to 400°F. Put the broth in an ovenproof saucepan and bring to a simmer. Slowly whisk in the polenta along with some black pepper, then turn off the heat. Cover and bake for 20 minutes, then remove the lid, stir through the Parmesan, and return to the oven, uncovered, for another 10 minutes. Spoon the tomatoes over the polenta and serve. Serves 4.

Grapefruit polenta cake

¾ cup + 2 tbsp. unsalted
    butter, softened
1½ cups superfine sugar
3 eggs
1¼ cups ground almonds
½ cup + 1 tbsp. polenta
2 tsp. baking powder
2 pink grapefruit

I've always liked bitter flavors. Grapefruit takes the place of lemon or orange in a simple polenta cake, which is especially good to brighten cold, dark days.

Preheat the oven to 350°F. In a large bowl, cream the butter and ¾ cup plus 2 tablespoons superfine sugar until light and fluffy. Beat in the eggs one at a time, making sure each is incorporated before adding the next. In a separate bowl, combine the ground almonds, polenta, and baking powder. Fold the dry mix into the wet, then stir in the zest and juice of 1 grapefruit. Pour into a lined 8-inch square baking pan, level the top, and bake for 40 minutes, or until a toothpick inserted into the center comes out clean.

Meanwhile, in a small bowl, combine the juice of 1 grapefruit with the remaining sugar. Once the cake is out of the oven, prick all over with a toothpick, then spoon over the grapefruit syrup. Let cool completely before cutting. Serves 10-12.

Polenta fries

1¼ cups vegetable broth
⅓ cup polenta
¼ cup Parmesan, grated
Handful flat-leaf parsley,
    chopped
Olive oil

Polenta fries are incredibly moreish; serve as a side or snack with tomato relish.

Bring the broth to a boil, then slowly pour in the polenta, whisking continuously until thickened—about 5 minutes. Stir in the Parmesan, a handful of chopped parsley, and a good grind of black pepper. Tip into a lined square or rectangular baking pan, and level the surface. Leave to cool, then transfer to the refrigerator to firm up—this will take up to an hour.

Preheat the oven to 400°F. Cut the solid polenta into fries and transfer to a lined baking sheet. Brush with a little oil on each side, then bake for 30 minutes, turning halfway through cooking, until crisp. Serves 2-3.

Polenta pastry

1 cup white spelt flour
2 tbsp. polenta
1 tsp. dried oregano
Red pepper flakes
¼ cup + 3 tbsp. unsalted
    butter, cubed
1 tbsp. olive oil

Roll this out for a savory galette, maybe filled with greens and ricotta.

In a large bowl, combine the flour, polenta, oregano, a pinch each of red pepper flakes and salt, and some black pepper. Rub in the butter, then mix in the oil and 2-3 tablespoons ice-cold water, and bring together—the dough will be quite sticky. Gather it up in your hands, wrap, and refrigerate for one hour. Makes a galette for 6.

Polenta and rosemary roast potatoes

2 lb. 3 oz. floury potatoes
    (e.g. Yukon Gold)
2 tbsp. olive oil
⅓ cup + 2 tbsp. polenta
2 tbsp. rosemary leaves,
    chopped

Parboiling the potatoes beforehand will ensure the insides are super fluffy.

Peel the potatoes and cut them into large chunks. Transfer to a saucepan, cover with cold water, season with salt, and bring to a boil. Simmer for 15 minutes, until just cooked through, then drain and leave to air dry for a few minutes.

While the potatoes are cooking, preheat the oven to 400°F. Put the oil in a roasting pan and heat in the oven for a few minutes. On a large plate, combine the polenta, rosemary, and a generous amount of salt and pepper. Roll each potato in the polenta to coat evenly, then tip them into the hot roasting pan, and toss in the hot oil. Spread out into a single layer, return the pan to the oven, and roast for 25 minutes. Turn them over and continue roasting for 30 minutes. Serves 4.

Roasted red bell peppers

Your shortcut to sauces, toppings, and more. These tender, smoky-sweet peppers, which have been roasted until charred and blistered on the outside, peeled, then stored in brine, are a real time-saver and somewhat underrated. You can prepare them however you like: whizz into a sauce; cut into strips and add to tarts or tortillas; chop and toss into salads, pan bakes, shakshuka, or pastas. Spanish piquillo peppers, meanwhile, are smaller, sweeter, and triangular (their name derives from the Spanish for "little beak"). Again, these can be eaten straight from the jar or used in salads and rice dishes, or stuffed with salt cod and potatoes or vegetables.

PAIR WITH	Chicken, salt cod, shrimp, eggs, nuts (walnuts, cashews), cheese (goat's, ricotta, feta), paprika, rice, quinoa, farro, gnocchi, orzo, and herbs (basil, parsley, mint).
TRANSFORM	With their small size and firm skin, piquillo peppers are prime for stuffing—try a combination of goat cheese, olive oil, and some salt and pepper.
HACK	These can be turned into a super-quick sauce by blending with olive oil, garlic, seasoning, and maybe a spice, like za'atar or chile. Loosen with pasta cooking water.

Red pepper and walnut pesto

1 jar (16 oz.) roasted red bell peppers, drained
1 garlic clove, minced
⅔ cup walnuts
2 tbsp. olive oil
⅓ cup Parmesan, grated
Handful parsley

If stirring this through pasta, be sure to add a good splash of the pasta cooking water when mixing to get a nice, glossy coating.

Roughly chop the red bell peppers and add to a food processor with the garlic and walnuts. Blitz until you've got a chunky paste, then, with the motor still running, pour in the olive oil. Add the Parmesan, a handful of parsley, and some seasoning, and pulse again. Serves 4–6.

Red pepper and mushroom quesadillas

1 tbsp. olive oil
1 garlic clove, minced
3½ cups mushrooms, cut into chunks
½ tsp. cilantro seeds
½ tsp. cumin seeds
½ tsp. oregano
1 tsp. paprika
3 roasted red bell peppers, roughly chopped
3 scallions, sliced
½ cup shredded Cheddar
2 tortillas

Quesadillas are such a quick meal and require little more than some guacamole or tomato salsa.

Heat the oil in a skillet over medium heat. Add the garlic and mushrooms, and cook until the mushrooms are browned and the liquid has evaporated. Season with salt. In a mortar, grind the cilantro and cumin seeds, then tip into the skillet along with the oregano and paprika. Stir and continue cooking for a minute or two, until fragrant. Tip the mushroom mix into a bowl and cool slightly.

Add the chopped bell peppers to a bowl, along with the scallions and Cheddar. Lay a tortilla on your countertop, spoon the mixture on top and spread evenly. Top with another tortilla. Heat a skillet and toast the quesadilla for a couple of minutes on each side. Serves 2.

Shrimp with peppers

1 onion, chopped
Glug of olive oil
1 green bell pepper, cut into chunks
2 garlic cloves, sliced
1 tsp. paprika
1 tbsp. tomato paste
6½ oz. raw, peeled jumbo shrimp, deveined
1 large roasted red pepper, chopped
Handful flat-leaf parsley, chopped
Squeeze of lemon

Don't be shy with the lemon juice here, and you'll want a good hunk of crusty bread to serve alongside.

Cook the onion in a good glug of olive oil until softened, then add the green pepper and garlic, and cook until softened. Add the paprika and tomato paste, cook for a minute, then add the shrimp and cook until they turn pink. Add the roasted red pepper and a pinch of salt, then continue cooking until the shrimp are cooked through. Serve scattered with the parsley, a squeeze of lemon, and a drizzle of olive oil. Serves 2.

Roast red pepper rice

1 tbsp. oil

1 large onion, finely sliced

2 garlic cloves, finely diced

1 jar (16 oz.) roasted red bell peppers, sliced

1⅓ cups basmati rice, rinsed

1 tbsp. tomato paste

3¼ cups broth

Large handful flat-leaf parsley, chopped

Half a lemon, juiced

4 scallions, sliced

This is super simple to bring together and will happily sit alongside white fish or chicken.

Heat the oil in a large skillet, then fry the onion until soft. Add the garlic, fry for another minute or so until fragrant, then stir in the bell peppers, and continue cooking for a couple of minutes. Tip in the rice and cook, stirring, for 2 minutes until the grains are coated.

Add the tomato paste, broth, parsley, and some salt and pepper. Once it starts to simmer, cover and cook, stirring occasionally, for 15 minutes until the rice is tender and the broth has been absorbed. Squeeze over the lemon juice, then tip into a bowl, and serve scattered with the scallions. Serves 4-6.

Flatbread with romesco, leeks, and ricotta

¾ cup whole shelled almonds

2 tsp. paprika

1 jar (16 oz.) roasted red bell peppers, drained

¼ cup dry bread crumbs

1 garlic clove, minced

1 tbsp. sherry vinegar

3 tbsp. olive oil

2 leeks

Pinch of red pepper flakes

2 flatbreads

¾ cup ricotta

You'll end up with more romesco than you need, but that's no bad thing. Use leftovers in sandwiches, pan bakes, as a dip or to accompany eggs.

Preheat the oven to 400°F and toast the almonds for 6 minutes. Whizz in a food processor, then add the paprika, peppers, bread crumbs, garlic, vinegar, olive oil, and some salt and pepper. Whizz again and set aside.

Cut the leeks into sticks, put on a baking sheet, and toss with a little oil and the red pepper flakes. Roast until completely soft. Spread romesco over the top of each flatbread, then dot with ricotta. Top with the leeks, season with black pepper, and bake for 2-4 minutes. Serves 2.

Chickpeas

These little chickpeas (aka garbanzo beans) get along with so many flavors, from warming spices (cumin, turmeric, cinnamon) to hot chiles, sweet tomatoes, and salty Parmesan, and are as happy in a salad as they are in stews. A stalwart of Mediterranean, Middle Eastern, and Indian cooking, chickpeas can do it all. Packed with protein, they are available in many forms: dried, precooked in cans and jars, and as flour. While cans and jars are, of course, the easier option, it's also worth considering using dried chickpeas. First, they'll need soaking, until doubled in size. Then transfer to a saucepan with twice the volume of (fresh) water, some baking soda, and any flavorings you like (bay or cumin, say), and cook until tender.

TRANSFORM	The smooth, salty nature of jarred chickpeas makes them ideal for producing silky hummus, with freshly squeezed lemon juice, garlic, and good-quality tahini.
HEALTH	High in protein, iron, and vitamin B, chickpeas are also a source of fiber.
HACK	Canned chickpeas also gives you aquafaba (aka chickpea water), which you can use to make vegan meringue, chocolate mousse, and cocktails, such as whiskey sours.

Chickpeas alla vodka

1½ tbsp. olive oil
1 red onion, finely sliced
1 garlic clove, crushed
1 cup sieved tomatoes
Pinch of red pepper flakes
½ tbsp. tomato paste
2 tbsp. vodka
¼ cup heavy cream
1 can (15½ oz.)chickpeas,
    drained and rinsed
Handful basil leaves

This vodka-spiked sauce is normally served with penne but do give chickpeas a chance.

Heat the oil in a large saucepan and fry the onion with a pinch of salt until softened. Add the garlic, fry for 2 more minutes, then add the sieved tomatoes, a good pinch of red pepper flakes, and the tomato paste. Bubble, stirring regularly, for 15 minutes, then add the vodka. Simmer for a few minutes more, then stir in the heavy cream (or plant-based equivalent). Add the chickpeas, then simmer for a few minutes to heat them through and until the sauce thickens. Season to taste and serve with torn basil leaves on top. Serves 2.

Simple chocolate mousse

1 cup + 2 tbsp. dark
    chocolate chips
½ cup chickpea water
    (drained from 1 x
    15½ oz. can chickpeas)
2 tbsp. golden honey
Berries, to serve

Consider this a blank canvas to customize as you see fit (with vanilla or sesame seeds, for example). It can easily be made vegan, too, by using sugar instead of golden honey.

Put the chocolate chips in a heatproof bowl over a saucepan of simmering water (be sure the bottom of the bowl doesn't touch the water). Once melted, remove from the heat and set aside to cool a little.

In a clean bowl, whisk the chickpea water (or aquafaba) until it starts to foam and you have stiff peaks—this will take about 15 minutes with a hand-held electric mixer. Gently fold a spoonful of aquafaba into the chocolate, then slowly add the rest until incorporated. Fold in the honey with a pinch of salt, then divide between four pots, and refrigerate for at least 1 hour. Serve topped with your favorite berries. Makes 4.

Roast spiced chickpeas

1 jar (11½ oz.) chickpeas,
    drained and rinsed
Drizzle of oil
½ tsp. ground cumin
½ tsp. smoked sweet
    paprika
½ tsp. sumac
Pinch of cayenne pepper

Keep a tub of these ready to top soups and salads, or simply to snack on.

Preheat the oven to 400°F. Line a baking sheet with aluminum foil. Pat dry the chickpeas, then toss with a little oil, the ground cumin, paprika, sumac, a pinch of cayenne pepper, and a pinch of salt. Roast for 25 minutes, stirring halfway through cooking, until crisp. Store in an airtight container. Serves 4.

Lemon, chickpea, and parsley orecchiette

1 jar (24¾ oz.) chickpeas, drained and liquid reserved

¼ cup olive oil

7 oz. orecchiette

3 garlic cloves, sliced

1 shallot, diced

Red pepper flakes

1 lemon, zested and juice of half

Large handful flat-leaf parsley, chopped

Knob of butter

⅓ cup Parmesan, grated

There are many versions of chickpeas and pasta, but this one is fresh, light, yet comforting thanks to its brothy state.

Pat the chickpeas dry in a clean kitchen towel. Heat 3 tablespoons oil in a heavy-bottomed saucepan, and fry the chickpeas, stirring occasionally, over medium heat until golden all over, 8-10 minutes. Transfer to a plate.

Cook the pasta in boiling salted water according to the package instructions. Meanwhile, add 1 tablespoon oil to the chickpea pan, add the garlic, and cook for a couple of minutes. Add the shallot, a good pinch each of red pepper flakes and salt, and cook until soft. Add 4 tablespoons chickpea water, bring to a simmer, and cook for a couple of minutes. Stir in the cooked pasta, along with the lemon zest, parsley, and a few splashes of the pasta cooking water. Toss in the fried chickpeas and a knob of butter, then finish with the lemon juice, lots of black pepper, the Parmesan, and a good drizzle of olive oil. Serve with more grated Parmesan if you like. Serves 2.

Tahini yogurt chickpeas with pickled red onion

1 red onion, thinly sliced

1 tbsp. red wine vinegar

Pinch of sugar

2 tbsp. tahini

⅜ cup Greek yogurt

1 lemon, juiced

1 jar (24¾ oz.) chickpeas, drained

½ tsp. sumac

Large handful cilantro leaves, torn

Drizzle of pomegranate molasses

These are so easy to pull together and make a great filler for pitta or baked sweet potatoes.

Put the onion in a small bowl and combine with the vinegar and a pinch each of salt and sugar. Scrunch everything together and set aside. In a large bowl, combine the tahini, yogurt, lemon juice, and some salt and pepper. Mix in the chickpeas and sumac, and tip onto a plate. Top with the pickled onion, cilantro, and a good drizzle of pomegranate molasses. Serves 4.

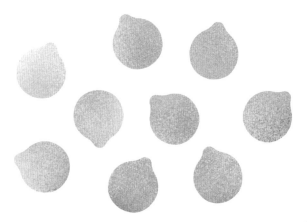

Harissa

Probably my favorite of the chile condiment world, harissa provides sweetness, smoke, and a hit of spice to anything it comes into contact with. The North African paste is (usually) made from dried chiles, spices, herbs, lemon, and sometimes garlic, while its rose version adds rose petals and sometimes rosewater for fragrance. Just a spoonful will add punch to roast vegetables, scrambled eggs, soups, couscous, stews, or marinades for meat or fish. Harissa also works a treat in place of ketchup on burgers, or combined with mayonnaise, ketchup, and lime juice for a retro shrimp cocktail.

PAIRS WITH	Chicken, shrimp, shrimp, salmon, cod, root vegetables, cauliflower, eggplant, cabbage, chickpeas, butter beans, halloumi, pomegranate, and honey.
TRANSFORM	Stir harissa through softened butter then slather over cooked corn on the cob.
HACK	The amount of harissa used is often up to you; taste and adjust to suit your chile taste.

Stuffed harissa tomatoes

¼ cup couscous
⅜ cup vegetable broth
2 beefsteak tomatoes
Glug of olive oil
1 small onion, chopped
2 garlic cloves, chopped
1 tbsp. harissa
Small handful mint, chopped
Small handful flat-leaf parsley, chopped
⅓ cup pine nuts

Stuffed tomatoes have a lot going for them: they couldn't be easier to make, can be served warm or at room temperature, and work with grilled fish, meat, salad, roast potatoes, or solo.

Put the couscous in a bowl and pour over the broth. Cover and set aside for 15 minutes. Meanwhile, cut the tops off the tomatoes then use a teaspoon to carefully spoon out the pulp and transfer to a sieve set over a bowl to drain. Chop the pulp.

Preheat the oven to 400°F. Heat a good glug of oil in a saucepan, then add the onion and garlic, and cook until softened. Add the chopped tomato pulp, and continue cooking until reduced and thickened, then stir in the harissa. Take off the heat, then stir in the mint and parsley, pine nuts, and some seasoning. Put the hollowed-out tomatoes on a lightly oiled baking dish and fill each one to the brim with couscous. Pop the lids on top, drizzle with oil, and bake for 25 minutes, until softened. Serves 2.

Sticky harissa chicken

4 chicken thighs
1 tbsp. rose harissa
1 tbsp. golden honey
1 garlic clove, crushed
½ tsp. ground cinnamon
Handful pistachios, chopped

Smoky from the harissa, sweet from the honey: just be sure to marinate the meat for at least 2 hours. Couscous would be a good accompaniment.

Put the chicken in a bowl skin-side down, fitting snugly. Mix the harissa, honey, garlic, and cinnamon in a small bowl, then tip half the mix over the chicken, making sure it's evenly coated. Turn the chicken skin-side up and pour over the remaining mix. Cover and put in the refrigerator for 2 hours.

Preheat the oven to 400°F. Transfer the chicken to a roasting dish, then bake skin-side up for 35 minutes, or until the skin is crisp and the meat cooked through. Leave to rest for 10 minutes, then serve scattered with chopped pistachios. Serves 2.

Harissa squash, carrot, and chickpea pan bake

2 cups carrots, cut into chunks
1 large red onion, cut into eighths
Half a butternut squash, cut into half-moons
3 tbsp. olive oil
1 tbsp. golden honey
1 tbsp. harissa
1 can (15½ oz.) chickpeas, drained, rinsed, and patted dry
½ cup yogurt
1 tbsp. tahini
Half a lemon, juiced
Handful mint, chopped
Sprinkling of dukkah

You want some crunch here, so the dukkah is important. If you can't find any, pomegranate seeds would be a good substitute.

Preheat the oven to 400°F. Put the carrots, onion, and butternut squash on a baking sheet. Add the oil, honey, harissa, and some salt and pepper, then mix to combine. Roast for 20 minutes, then mix in the chickpeas, and continue cooking for 20 minutes. Meanwhile, in a small bowl combine the yogurt, tahini, lemon juice, mint, and a pinch of salt. Serve the pan bake topped with the yogurt and a sprinkling of dukkah. Serves 4.

Harissa frittata with herbs and feta

1 tbsp. olive oil
1 onion, thinly sliced
1 tbsp. harissa
6 eggs, lightly whisked
Large handful cilantro, chopped
1 tbsp. nigella seeds
⅔ cup feta

A frittata which welcomes something green alongside, like a peppery arugula salad.

Heat the oil in an ovenproof skillet. Add the onion and cook, stirring occasionally, until caramelized. Transfer the onions to a bowl, then add the harissa, eggs, cilantro, nigella seeds, and some seasoning. Pour the lot into the pan, crumble over the feta, and put over a low heat until the outside and bottom are set—about 6 minutes. Transfer to a hot broiler and cook until golden, about 3 minutes. Serves 2.

Harissa cheese straws

12 oz. sheet puff pastry
Flour, for dusting
2 tbsp. rose harissa
1 cup shredded Cheddar
1 egg, whisked

Few things bring more joy than a cheese straw with a cocktail, and harissa brings a subtle heat to the party.

Preheat the oven to 425°F. Unroll the pastry on a lightly floured countertop. Spread the harissa over the top half of the pastry then scatter over ½ cup Cheddar. Fold up the bottom half of the pastry, then roll out slightly to around ¼-inch thickness. Trim the ends then slice into ¾-inch strips. Gently twist each strip 3 or 4 times, then lay on a lined baking sheet, leaving space between each one. Brush each strip with egg wash and scatter with the remaining Cheddar. Bake for 15 minutes, until golden. Leave to cool. Makes 20.

Bread crumbs

Most meals can be improved with a sprinkling of bread crumbs: fried until biscuity and used to top pasta; spread out on a plate to form part of the triple dip alongside flour and egg to coat chicken breast or fish; stirred through meat or vegetables to bind burgers or fritters. Of course, you can make bread crumbs yourself by whizzing any leftover loaves and storing in the freezer. The bonus of this route (other than preventing food waste) is that you can add extra oomph by flavoring with whatever takes your fancy, be it garlic, herbs, chile, Parmesan, lemon, anchovies, or za'atar.

VARIETIES	Bread crumbs can be fresh or dried and vary in texture. Panko, which originate from Asia, come in two varieties (white, made from crustless bread, and tan, from the entire loaf), are flakier and don't absorb as much oil so are lighter once fried (use for things like chicken tenders or fish sticks). Fresh, meanwhile, have not been dried and are soft in texture (use as a binder in meatballs, in the filling of a treacle tart, or bread sauce); dried are used to coat ingredients, like fish, before frying, or to top a gratin or macaroni cheese.
TRANSFORM	Mix things up by whizzing rye bread into crumbs, combining with sugar and spices (think cinnamon), and baking or toasting in a skillet. Fold through desserts, such as parfait, crumble, or trifle.
HACK	For even-size fresh bread crumbs, whizz sliced bread in a processor until you have your desired size, then push them through a coarse sieve.

パン粉

PANKO

Zucchini parmigiana

This lives or dies by removing as much water from the zucchini as possible, so don't skip the first step.

6 zucchini
Glug of olive oil
1 onion, diced
2 garlic cloves, diced
1 bunch basil, stalks chopped, leaves torn
2 cans (14½ oz. each) tomatoes
1⅔ cups mozzarella, sliced
½ cup Parmesan, grated
½ cup dry bread crumbs

Use a mandolin or peeler to cut the zucchini into ¼-inch slices, and transfer to a bowl. Sprinkle with salt and set aside for 15 minutes, then pat dry with paper towels. Heat a good glug of olive oil in a saucepan over medium heat. Add the onion and cook until softened. Add the garlic and chopped basil stalks, then fry gently for 2 minutes. Add the tomatoes and cook, stirring occasionally, for 25 minutes. Stir in a handful of basil leaves and season.

Preheat the oven to 350°F. In a skillet, char the zucchini slices for a few minutes on each side—you will need to do this in batches. Put a third of the tomato sauce in a baking dish, then cover with a third of the zucchini, a few torn basil leaves, and a third of both cheeses. Repeat the layers twice more, mixing the final tablespoon of Parmesan with the bread crumbs and a drizzle of oil. Sprinkle this over the top and bake for 25 minutes. Serves 8.

Miso mushroom sausage rolls

My uncle Ron makes the best meat-free sausage rolls (a take on Delia Smith's Christmas classic), but these, with some much-needed umami from the miso, come a close second.

1 tbsp. olive oil
1 onion, finely diced
1 celery stalk, finely diced
2 garlic cloves, crushed
3¼ cups cremini mushrooms, finely chopped
1 tsp. thyme leaves
2 tsp. brown rice miso
1 tsp. Dijon mustard
1⅓ cups fresh bread crumbs
⅓ cup cooked chestnuts, chopped
12 oz. sheet puff pastry
Milk, for glazing

Heat the oil in a skillet, then cook the onion and celery until golden—about 10 minutes. Add the garlic, mushrooms, and thyme, and cook, stirring occasionally, for another 10 minutes. Stir in the miso and mustard and cook for a few more minutes. Tip the lot into a bowl and leave to cool. Stir in the bread crumbs and chestnuts, and season generously with black pepper.

Preheat the oven to 400°F. Put the puff pastry on a lightly floured countertop, roll out slightly, then cut in half lengthwise. Spoon half the mushroom mix along the middle of one long length of pastry and mold it into a sausage shape. Bring one side of pastry over the filling, pressing the edges with a fork to seal. Slice on the diagonal into eight pieces, then repeat with the remaining pastry and mushroom mix. Transfer the rolls to a lined baking sheet, brush each one with milk, and bake for 20-25 minutes, until golden brown. Makes 16.

Plum brown betty

1 cup dry bread crumbs

3 tbsp. brown sugar

1 tsp. pumpkin pie spice

⅓ cup + 1 tsp. unsalted butter, melted

1¾ lb. plums, pitted and cut into sixths

⅛ cup superfine sugar

Half a lemon, zested and juiced

1 tbsp. cornstarch

A cousin of the crumble and cobbler, but topped with sweetened, spiced bread crumbs instead. Serve with vanilla ice cream.

Preheat the oven to 425°F. In a bowl, combine the bread crumbs, brown sugar, and pumpkin pie spice, then mix in the melted butter. Put the plums, superfine sugar, lemon zest and juice, and cornstarch in a bowl and combine. Tip into a baking dish and top with the bread crumbs. Cover with aluminum foil and bake for 20 minutes, then remove the foil and bake for another 20 minutes. Serves 6-8.

Carrot top gremolata

Extra virgin olive oil

½ cup dry bread crumbs

1 lemon, zested

1 garlic clove, crushed

2 large handfuls carrot tops, chopped

Gremolata, the Italian condiment usually made from parsley, lemon, and garlic, makes all pasta and vegetable dishes taste better. Here, I've swapped parsley for carrot tops.

Heat a little olive oil in a skillet over medium heat, then add the bread crumbs and toast, stirring regularly, until golden brown and smelling like graham crackers. Take off the heat, stir through the lemon zest, the garlic, and carrot tops, and season with salt and pepper. Serves 4.

Crispy haddock and watercress bread rolls

⅓ cup all-purpose flour

1 egg, beaten

⅔ cup panko bread crumbs

1 lemon, zested and juiced

1 tsp. dried oregano

9 oz. haddock fillets, cut into fat strips

2 tbsp. oil

4 bread rolls

Tartare sauce

Handful watercress

Sliced gherkins or cornichons would make an excellent addition.

Put the flour on one plate, the egg on another, and bread crumbs on a third. Season the flour and add the lemon zest and oregano. Dip a haddock strip into the flour, shake off any excess, then dip into the egg, followed by the bread crumbs. Repeat with the other fish strips and refrigerate for 10 minutes.

Heat 1 tablespoon oil in a large skillet and, once hot, fry half the fish until golden on all sides. Drain on kitchen towel, then repeat with the other half of the fish and 1 tablespoon oil. Once cooked, squeeze over the juice of half a lemon. Slice the bread rolls in half and toast. Spread each base with tartare sauce, then top with the fish and watercress. Top with the lid. Serves 4.

Mango chutney

Chutneys can really make a meal sing, with mango being a prime example. Sweet, aromatic, and with pleasing chunks of the golden fruit, this Indian condiment is one of the go-to accompaniments for curries or for dipping papadams. Often the unplanned addition that we never regret, mango chutney is such a quick way to bring vibrancy to weeknight flavors, whether in a glaze for meats, mixed into a dressing, or my personal favorite: simply spread in a grilled cheese sandwich (it's also good paired with a cheeseboard).

PAIR WITH	Chicken, pork, cold ham, game, shrimp, curries, potato, carrot, cauliflower, celeriac, chickpeas, Cheddar, paneer, yogurt, and cashews.
TRANSFORM	Pep up cheese straws for a party by spreading a couple of tablespoons of mango chutney on the pastry before adding the shredded Cheddar.
HACK	Swirl a teaspoon of mango chutney through yogurt for an instant accompaniment to curries.

Cheese and chutney English muffins

⅓ cup shredded Cheddar
2 scallions, thinly sliced
½ tsp. nigella seeds
2 tsp. mango chutney
2 English muffins

Mango chutney and cheese are great friends, especially when brought together to top an English muffin.

In a bowl, combine the Cheddar, scallions, and nigella seeds. Spread the mango chutney on the muffins and top with the cheese mix. Put under the grill until the cheese has melted. Serves 2.

Pea and potato pakoras

1¾ cups potatoes, diced
¾ cup frozen peas
1 cup chickpea (garbanzo) flour
1 tsp. garam masala
1 tsp. turmeric
1 tsp. black mustard seeds
1 small red onion, diced
1 red chile, diced
Drizzle of oil
Mango chutney
A few cilantro leaves

These can easily be sized up for a more substantial meal, or down to serve as a party snack.

Cook the diced potato in a saucepan of boiling salted water for about 8 minutes until tender, adding the peas in the last minute. Drain and leave to cool a little.

In a bowl, mix the chickpea flour with the garam masala, turmeric, black mustard seeds, and some salt and pepper. Add the red onion, red chile, and the potato and peas. Slowly add ½ cup water until you have a batter. Heat a little oil in a skillet, then fry spoonfuls of the potato mix on each side until golden. Spread a little mango chutney on top of each one, plus a cilantro leaf. Makes 6-8.

Coronation chickpeas

2 tbsp. mango chutney
3 tbsp. yogurt
1–1½ tsp. mild curry powder (depending on preference)
Half a lime, juiced
1 jar (11½ oz.) chickpeas, drained and rinsed
⅓ cup golden raisins
Handful cilantro, chopped

Memories of coronation chicken might not be great ones, but this version, which uses chickpeas and yogurt, makes a great sandwich filler or addition to a romaine lettuce salad.

In a bowl, combine the chutney, yogurt, curry powder, and lime juice. Mix in the chickpeas, golden raisins, and cilantro, and season. Serve in a sandwich alongside baby spinach, or as a salad with crunchy lettuce. Serves 2 as part of a salad, or 4 as a sandwich filler.

Sticky mango chicken and potatoes

1 lb. 3½ oz. baby potatoes, cut in half
2 tbsp. olive oil
1 tbsp. curry powder
Pinch of red pepper flakes
5 tbsp. mango chutney
1 tbsp. lemon juice
1 tsp. cumin seeds
4 chicken breasts
Handful cilantro

You could eat this on its own, or as part of a spread with naan bread, yogurt, and something green, like peas or spinach.

Preheat the oven to 400°F and pop a roasting pan inside. Boil the potatoes in a saucepan of salted water for 6 minutes. Drain and leave in the colander for a few minutes to air dry. Tip the potatoes onto the hot baking sheet, toss with 1 tablespoon of the olive oil, curry powder, and red pepper flakes, and roast for 10 minutes.

Meanwhile, combine the chutney with the lemon juice, cumin seeds, and 1 tablespoon olive oil, and use to liberally coat the chicken. Once the potatoes have had their 10 minutes, nestle the chicken among them, and cook for another 25 minutes until the meat is cooked through. Serve scatted with cilantro. Serves 4.

Mango chutney paneer with spinach

1 cup paneer
1 tsp. turmeric
1 tbsp. mango chutney
2 tsp. tomato paste
1 red chile, chopped
Knob of ginger, grated
2 garlic cloves, crushed
Large handful cilantro, chopped
1 tbsp. olive oil, plus some for cooking
2 handfuls spinach

If the weather is playing nice, thread onto skewers and grill on the barbecue.

Cut the paneer into cubes and add to a bowl along with all the ingredients (except the spinach). Season, give everything a good stir, and set aside for 1 hour. Heat a little oil in a skillet, then cook the paneer, turning, until grilled on each side—about 6 minutes. Add the spinach, stirring until wilted. Serves 2-3.

Dried mushrooms

The mushroom kingdom is an enchanting and varied one. Whether porcini, shiitake, morels, chanterelles, or a mix of wild, dried mushrooms have so much to offer. Small and unassuming, they pack a lot of flavor, bringing a rich, savory back note to stews, broths, and ragus, while lending a meaty texture. Yes, they are expensive, but just a few will result in a welcoming umami punch. Rehydrate dried mushrooms by placing them in a bowl and covering with plenty of hot water. You'll not only get the mushrooms, but the wonderfully rich soaking liquid too, which will need straining to get rid of any grit.

VARIETIES	Utilize shiitake in gravies, broths, and stir-fries; the highly prized morels or porcini in risotto; and wild mushrooms in stews (particularly beef or chicken).
PAIRS WITH	Beef, chicken, pork, sausages, fresh mushrooms, root vegetables, onions, fennel, tomatoes, nuts, pasta, rice, butter beans, rosemary, parsley, Parmesan, and goat cheese.
HACK	Blitz a handful of porcini until a fine powder, then add to soups and ragus, or sprinkle on steaks.

Cauliflower and mushroom Bolognese

Cauliflower and mushrooms lend a satisfying meaty texture, while the pasta brings all the carb comfort.

¾ cup dried porcini mushrooms

2⅔ cups cremini mushrooms, stalks removed

1 medium cauliflower, cut into florets

2 tbsp. olive oil

1 onion, finely chopped

2 garlic cloves, finely sliced

Red pepper flakes

1 tsp. chopped rosemary

4 tbsp. tomato paste

14 oz. pasta (e.g., spaghetti, rigatoni)

¼ cup Parmesan, grated

Half a lemon, zested

Put the porcini in a bowl, pour over boiling water to cover, and leave to soak while you get on with the rest. Blitz the mushrooms in a food processor then transfer to a bowl. Roughly chop the cauliflower florets and blitz until they resemble rice; set aside. Heat the oil in a saucepan and fry the onion until soft. Add the garlic, a pinch of red pepper flakes, and the rosemary, and cook until the garlic has softened. Add the tomato paste, cook for a couple more minutes, then add the blitzed mushrooms and cauliflower, and season. Cook, stirring occasionally, for 10 minutes.

Meanwhile, cook the pasta in salted boiling water until al dente. Transfer the pasta to the sauce, add the Parmesan, lemon zest, and a splash of pasta cooking water to loosen. Combine and season if needed. Eat with more grated Parmesan over the top. Serves 4.

Peppercorn mushrooms

Spoon over butter bean mash: heat a little oil in a saucepan, add a crushed garlic clove, cook for a minute, then add a jar or can of butter beans, 2 tablespoons water, and 1½ tablespoons lemon juice. Mash, season, and warm through.

⅓ cup dried porcini mushrooms

4 portabello mushrooms

Olive oil, for brushing

1 tsp. crushed green peppercorns

⅜ cup white wine

2 garlic cloves, finely chopped

1 shallot, finely diced

2 tbsp. sour cream

1 tsp. Dijon mustard

In a small bowl, soak the porcini in 1 cup boiling water for 15 minutes, then chop. Meanwhile, remove the stems and gills (using a spoon) from the portobellos. Brush the mushrooms with oil and sprinkle with the peppercorns. Put a skillet over medium heat, then add the mushrooms gill-side up, pressing down with a spatula. Cook until browned, about 6 minutes, then flip and cook on the other side for 5 minutes, again pressing down. Transfer the mushrooms to a plate.

Add the wine to the pan, then once it has reduced a little, add the garlic, shallot, porcini and its soaking liquid, and a pinch of salt. Once the shallot is cooked and the sauce thickened, stir in the sour cream and mustard, and warm through. To serve, spoon the sauce over the peppercorn mushrooms. Serves 2.

Mushroom broth

1⅓ cups dried shiitake
   mushrooms
1 tbsp. sesame oil
2 garlic cloves, finely chopped
Thumb-size piece of ginger,
   minced
Half a red chile, finely
   chopped
2 scallions, finely sliced
2½ cups broth
1 tbsp. soy sauce
Half a lime, juiced

If you have any cooked chicken, shred, then toss it in.

Soak the shiitake in 1 cup boiling water for 20 minutes. Heat the oil
in a saucepan, then add the garlic, ginger, red chile, and scallions.
Cook for a couple of minutes until fragrant, then add the rehydrated
mushrooms and cook for another 5 or so minutes, until everything
is nice and soft. Add the broth and mushroom soaking liquid and
bring to a boil. Season with the soy sauce and lime juice. Serves 2.

Mushroom and bok choi noodle soup

Mushroom broth
   (see above)
7 oz. soba noodles
3 bok choi, leaves shredded
Scallions, sliced,
   to serve
Sesame seeds, to serve

**Make more of a meal of the mushroom broth (above) by
adding noodles and greens.**

Make the mushroom broth. Cook the soba noodles according to the
package instructions, then drain and rinse under cold water. Divide
the noodles between two bowls. Add the bok choi to the broth and
continue cooking until tender. Pour the broth over the noodles and
garnish with sliced scallions and sesame seeds. Serves 2.

Mushroom and spinach spelt

⅓ cup dried wild
   mushrooms or porcini
4 cups broth
2 tbsp. olive oil
1 garlic clove, sliced
2 leeks, sliced
¾ cup spelt
1 bay leaf
⅜ cup white wine
2⅔ cups cremini
   mushrooms, sliced
5 cups spinach
¼ cup Parmesan, grated

**This is cooked in the same way you would a risotto but uses
spelt, which brings a nice nuttiness.**

Soak the mushrooms in ½ cup boiling water for 15 minutes. Chop
the soaked mushrooms and tip the soaking liquid into a saucepan
with the broth and gently simmer.

   Heat 1 tablespoon oil in a heavy-bottomed saucepan and cook
the garlic and leeks until softened. Stir in the spelt and bay leaf,
cooking for a minute or two until well coated, then add the wine
and cook until evaporated. Start adding the broth a ladleful at a
time, waiting for it to be absorbed before adding the next spoonful.
Keep going until the spelt is cooked—about 30 minutes. Meanwhile,
heat 1 tablespoon oil in a skillet and fry the sliced mushrooms and
soaked mushrooms until golden. Stir in the spinach until wilted,
then season. Once the spelt is cooked, mix in the vegetables. Add
the Parmesan, stir again, then check the seasoning. Serves 2.

Dark chocolate

Chocolate is deeply personal but, for me, when it comes to cooking it must be bittersweet. Always use the best quality you can and steer clear of "baking chocolate"—although it seems counterintuitive, this usually contains added oils and fats, so it's much less reliable and likely to split when melting for, say, a ganache. I go for 70% cocoa solids but, again, this comes down to preference, and opting for bars of chocolate over chocolate chips will give you more options: keep your chocolate chunkier, chop into smaller pieces, or go for uniform or uneven sizes.

PAIRS WITH	Bourbon, chestnut, cherry, orange, pear, passion fruit, blood orange, berries, banana, prune, hazelnut, peanut, walnut, hazelnut, pistachio, caramel, mint, bay, chile, black pepper, miso, ginger, coffee, rye, venison, and mushroom.
HEALTH	Rich in antioxidants and polyphenols, dark chocolate also contains minerals, such as magnesium, zinc, and iron.
TRANSFORM	While dark chocolate can do no wrong in cakes and cookies, it can add another dimension to savory dishes—try using a square or two in chili con carne or mole.

Mushroom chili

1 large white onion, chopped
2 garlic cloves, chopped
1 red chile, chopped
1 tsp. cumin seeds
1 tsp. paprika
1 tsp. dried oregano
Splash of oil
1 large carrot, finely chopped
2⅔ cups cremini mushrooms, cut into chunks
1 can (14 oz.) kidney beans, drained and rinsed
1 can (14½ oz.) chopped tomatoes
2 tbsp. dark chocolate
Squeeze of lemon juice
1 small handful cilantro leaves, chopped

The chocolate adds a real depth of flavor to this vegetable chili. Eat with rice or quinoa and a spoonful of yogurt.

Cook the onion, garlic, chile, cumin seeds, paprika, and oregano in a splash of oil, stirring occasionally, for 5 minutes. Add the carrots, cook for a few minutes, then add the mushrooms and continue cooking for another 2 minutes. Tip in the beans, tomatoes, and 1 cup water, then simmer for 20-25 minutes, until thickened. Stir in the chocolate, followed by a squeeze of lemon juice, some seasoning, and the cilantro. Serves 3-4.

Chocolate and coffee crinkle cookies

3 tbsp. + 2 tsp unsalted butter, cubed
½ cup + 1 tbsp. dark chocolate, broken up
1 egg
¼ cup superfine sugar
⅓ cup light brown sugar, packed
½ cup dark rye flour
½ tsp. baking soda
¼ cup unsweetened cocoa powder
1 tsp. ground coffee
Confectioners' sugar, to coat

Leave ample space between the cookies on the cookie sheet as these will spread.

Melt the butter and chocolate in a bowl set over (but not touching) a saucepan of simmering water; remove and leave the mix to cool a little. Meanwhile, whisk the egg and sugars in a bowl until pale and thick, then stir in the melted chocolate. Add the flour, baking powder, cocoa powder, coffee, and a pinch of salt, and combine. Cover and put in the refrigerator for 1 hour. Preheat the oven to 350°F. Roll the dough into eight balls, then roll each one in confectioners' sugar to coat and transfer to a lined cookie sheet. Bake for 13-15 minutes, until the edges are firm. Cool for 10 minutes on the sheet before transferring to a wire rack to cool completely. Makes 8.

Flourless chocolate, pear, and hazelnut cake

½ cup + 1 tbsp. dark chocolate, broken up

¼ cup + 3 tbsp. butter, cubed

3 eggs, separated

⅔ cup + 1 tbsp. hazelnuts, roasted then ground

⅓ cup + 2 tbsp. light brown sugar

3 pears, peeled, halved and sliced

Roast the hazelnuts in the oven for 10 minutes, before transferring to a food processor to grind finely.

Melt the chocolate, butter, and a pinch of salt in a bowl set over (but not touching) a saucepan of water. Set aside for a few minutes to cool, then stir in the egg yolks followed by the hazelnuts. Preheat the oven to 375°F. In a large, clean bowl, whisk the egg whites and sugar until soft peaks form. Stir a couple of spoonfuls into the chocolate mix, then fold in the rest. Spoon the mix into a lined 8-inch square pan, and top with the sliced pears. Bake for 30-40 minutes, until a toothpick inserted into the center of the cake comes out clean. Serves 9-12.

Chocolate drizzled ginger madeleines

¼ cup + 3 tbsp. butter, softened, plus extra for greasing

½ cup superfine sugar

2 eggs

¾ cup + 2½ tsp. self-rising flour

1 tsp. ground ginger

¼ tsp. cinnamon

1 tsp. vanilla extract

½ cup + 1 tbsp. dark chocolate, broken up

I like to drizzle these with melted chocolate, but they would also be nice half dipped in chocolate.

Preheat the oven to 425°F. Grease a madeleine pan with melted butter. Then, in a bowl, beat the butter and sugar until fluffy, then whisk in the eggs. Stir in the flour, ginger, cinnamon, and vanilla extract, then spoon the mix into the prepared pan. Bake for 10-12 minutes until golden brown around the edges. Turn the madeleines out onto a wire rack, and cool completely. Meanwhile, melt the chocolate in a bowl set over (but not touching) a saucepan of simmering water. Drizzle the chocolate over the madeleines and leave to set. Makes 8.

Spiced hot chocolate

1 cup milk of your choice

3 tbsp. good-quality dark chocolate

Pinch of ground cardamom

Pinch of ground cinnamon

Squirt of golden honey

For an after-dinner mint vibe, swap half the dark chocolate for mint dark chocolate.

Heat the milk in a saucepan, but make sure it doesn't boil. Whisk in the chocolate and spices, until the chocolate has melted. Add a squirt of honey, to taste, and pour into a mug. Serves 1.

Oats

Oats have a lot going for them: they're nourishing, filling, and good value. They are the main player in porridge and, for some, in crumbles, but they also present so many other possibilities, both sweet and savory. Oats are processed by rolling or steel-cutting, with the latter taking longer to cook. Rolled oats are very at home in porridge, granola, flapjacks, and cookies, or used to absorb moisture. Jumbo oats have a slightly nutty flavor and work in porridge and flapjacks, as well as granola, or incorporated into a soda bread dough (and sprinkled on top before baking). Pinhead, which are the roughest type of oats, are best used in stuffing or as a coating for fish and meat. Oatmeal should be reserved for crackers, parkin, or haggis, if the mood takes you.

TRANSFORM	Whizz oats in a food processor and use to encase oily fish, such as mackerel, or blitz them to a fine powder and use in place of flour for pancakes and waffles.
HEALTH	Oats provide micronutrients (copper, B vitamins, zinc), and are rich in prebiotic fibers, which can support gut health, and beta-glucan, which can be beneficial in managing blood sugar levels.
HACK	To add more flavor, toast your oats first—this will make all the difference to oat and raisin cookies.

Banana and oat pancakes

1 cup rolled oats
2 ripe bananas
1 tsp. ground cinnamon
½ tsp. vanilla extract
1 tsp. baking powder
2 eggs
Butter, for cooking

Serve with natural yogurt and a handful of blueberries.

In a food processor, whizz the oats, bananas, cinnamon, vanilla extract, baking powder, eggs, and a pinch of salt. Leave to rest for 15 minutes, until thickened slightly.

Heat a nonstick skillet over medium heat. Add a knob of butter then, once melted, add a couple of spoonfuls of batter for each pancake and cook in batches until bubbles appear and the bottom is set. Flip and cook on the other side for 1 minute. Repeat with the remaining batter. Makes 8 pancakes.

Carrot cake overnight oats

2¼ cups rolled oats
2 carrots, grated
⅓ cup raisins
2 tsp. ground cinnamon
1 tsp. nutmeg
1 tbsp. golden honey
¼ cup yogurt
Walnuts, chopped

**The flavors of a classic carrot cake in breakfast form.
You could always add some grated apple, too.**

In a large bowl, combine the oats, carrots, raisins, cinnamon, nutmeg, honey, and 2¼ cups water. Divide between four bowls, cover, and leave overnight. The next day, stir 1 tablespoon yogurt into each bowl and serve with chopped walnuts. Serves 4.

Oat and rosemary crackers

½ cup oats
¾ cup whole-wheat flour
1 tsp. baking powder
1 tsp. ground black pepper
1 tbsp. superfine sugar
1 tsp. chopped rosemary
3 tbsp. + 2 tsp. butter
    unsalted butter, cubed
2–3 tbsp. milk

**These would make a great addition to a cheeseboard or
packed up as a gift.**

In a bowl, rub together the oats, flour, baking powder, black pepper, sugar, rosemary, and butter, until you have a rough crumble. Add milk a tablespoon at a time to bring the dough together.

Preheat the oven to 375°F. Roll out the dough on a lightly floured countertop to a thickness of ¼ inch. Cut into ten rectangles and transfer to a lined baking sheet. Brush with a little milk or egg wash, sprinkle with salt, and bake for 15 minutes. Makes 10 crackers.

Blackberry, apple, and thyme crumble bars

2 cups all-purpose flour

⅓ cup + 2 tbsp. light brown sugar

1 cup rolled oats

¾ cup + 3 tbsp. unsalted butter, cubed

2 cups + 1 tablespoon blackberries

1 cup diced apple

3 tbsp. + 1tsp. superfine sugar

1 tsp. cornstarch

Half a lemon, zested and juiced

1 tsp. chopped thyme

The apples and blackberries cook down to a jammy consistency, while the thyme adds fragrance to the crumble topping.

Preheat the oven to 400°F. Line a 8-inch square baking pan with parchment paper, leaving an overhang. In a bowl, combine the flour, light brown sugar, and oats. Rub in the butter until you have coarse bread crumbs. Press a third of the mix into the baking pan and bake until golden, about 15 minutes. Put the remaining mixture in the refrigerator.

In a bowl, combine the blackberries, apple, superfine sugar, cornstarch, lemon zest and juice. Spoon over the baked base. Remove the reserved crumble from the refrigerator and stir through the thyme. Scatter over the fruit, then bake for 40 minutes until the fruit has softened and the top is golden. Allow to cool before slicing into bars. Makes 12 bars.

Prune and oat scones

1 cup prunes

½ cup Earl Grey tea

2 cups + 1 tbsp. spelt flour

1 tsp. baking powder

1 tsp. baking soda

¼ cup + 3 tbsp. unsalted butter, cubed

⅔ cup rolled oats, plus extra for sprinkling

⅞ cup buttermilk

Milk, for brushing

These scones are more savory than sweet, so eat for breakfast or as a snack with cheese.

Soak the prunes in the tea for 30 minutes, then cut them in half. Meanwhile, in a large bowl combine the flour, baking powder, baking soda, and a pinch of salt. Rub in the butter, then add the oats, buttermilk, and prunes, and bring everything together. Tip onto a lightly floured countertop and cut into eight triangles. Transfer the scones to a lined cookie sheet, brush with milk, and sprinkle with more oats. Bake at 425°F for about 15 minutes, until golden and puffed up. Makes 8 scones.

Green lentils

Enduring and dependable, green lentils are especially valuable in the cooler months. Bringing instant comfort—and quickly— the talent of the green lentil spans the globe, from the Middle East, to India, to Europe. With a mild flavor and soft texture, it's the pulse that has never let me down, bulking up soups, stews, and salads, or providing a filling for pies or stuffing vegetables, and a quick "Bolognese" when the refrigerator is bare. As with chickpeas, you could cook up a big batch of dried ones to see you through the week, or open a can, to make life easier.

PAIR WITH	Salmon, cod, chicken, pork chop, sausages, duck, fennel, spinach, sweet potato, tomato, spinach, capers, and balsamic vinegar.
TRANSFORM	Drained canned lentils will bulk out fritters nicely. Keep things green by combining with grated zucchini, scallions, and herbs, like mint.
HEALTH	A good source of plant-based protein, lentils are also rich in iron and fiber.

Herby lentil soup

2 tbsp. olive oil
2 large onions, sliced
3 garlic cloves, crushed
1 large bunch flat-leaf
   parsley, chopped
1 large bunch cilantro, chopped
1 large bunch dill, chopped
1 large bunch chives, chopped
2 tsp. paprika
3 tbsp. tomato paste
4 cups broth
1 can (15 oz.) green lentils,
   drained
Squeeze of lemon
Scallion, sliced

This is based on the Persian soup aash but is by no means traditional. You want a lot of herbs here, so when you think you've got enough, add a few more.

Heat the olive oil in a heavy-bottomed saucepan and cook the onions with a pinch of salt until caramelized. Stir in the garlic, cooking until fragrant, then add the herbs. Stir in the paprika, tomato paste, broth, and lentils, and simmer for 20 minutes. Season with black pepper and a good squeeze of lemon juice. Spoon into bowls and top with sliced scallion. Serves 6.

Eggplant polpette

2 tbsp. olive oil
1 eggplant, diced
1 onion, diced
1 tsp. pine nuts
1 garlic clove, crushed
1 tsp. tomato paste
½ tsp. paprika
1 lemon, zested
⅓ cup ready-cooked
   puy lentils
1 tbsp. capers, drained and
   rinsed
Handful basil
3 tbsp. fresh bread crumbs

Crisp, meat-free polpette, asking to be served with salads or spaghetti and tomato sauce.

Heat the oil in a heavy-bottomed skillet. Add the eggplant and cook, stirring occasionally, for 5 minutes. Add the onion and a pinch of salt and cook, stirring every now and then, for 15 minutes until the eggplant is soft and the onions are starting to brown.

Preheat the oven to 400°F. Add the pine nuts, garlic, tomato paste, paprika, and the lemon zest, and combine. Cook for a couple of minutes, then transfer to a food processor and blitz with the lentils, capers, and basil—you're looking for a chunky texture. Transfer to a bowl and stir through the bread crumbs. Divide into eight balls and bake on a lined baking sheet for 20–25 minutes. Makes 8 polpette.

Roast fennel, lentils, and salsa verde

3 fennel bulbs, trimmed and cut into thick wedges
Handful cherry tomatoes
1 lemon
1 bay leaf
Olive oil
1 garlic clove
1 tbsp. capers, drained and rinsed
1 large handful flat-leaf parsley, chopped
1 large handful basil, torn
1 can (15 oz.) green lentils, drained

You could top this with goat cheese, if you like, or to make it more substantial serve alongside fish, such as salmon.

Preheat the oven to 375°F. Put the fennel in a roasting pan with the tomatoes, three fat strips of lemon peel, the bay leaf, some seasoning, and 2 tablespoons olive oil. Give everything a good mix, then roast for 20 minutes.

Meanwhile, crush the garlic clove in a mortar, then stir in the capers, parsley, basil, and the juice of half the lemon. Season, add 1 tablespoon olive oil, and mix. Toss the lentils into the roast fennel along with the salsa verde. Return to the oven for 15 minutes. Serves 2–3.

Lentil lasagne

1 tbsp. olive oil
3 leeks, chopped
Red pepper flakes
2 garlic cloves, crushed
1½ cups chopped kale
2 cans (14½ oz. each) chopped tomatoes
1 can (15 oz.) green lentils, drained
1 lemon, zested
1 large handful basil, torn
1¾ cups mozzarella, torn
9 oz. fresh lasagne sheets

This is a cheat's version of lasagne, leaning heavily on cans for ease and speed.

Heat the oil in a saucepan, add the leeks and a pinch each of salt and red pepper flakes, and cook for 10 minutes until soft. Add the garlic, cook for another minute, then add the kale and continue cooking until wilted. Add the tomatoes, green lentils, lemon zest, and basil.

Preheat the oven to 400°F. Spoon a quarter of the sauce into an ovenproof dish. Scatter over a quarter of the mozzarella, then top with fresh lasagne sheets. Keep layering until everything is used up, finishing with a layer of mozzarella. Tear over some more fresh basil, drizzle with oil, then bake for 25–30 minutes until bubbling. Serves 4.

Moussaka bowls

1–2 tbsp. olive oil
1 onion, finely chopped
2 garlic cloves, crushed
1 tsp. cinnamon
2 tsp. oregano
1 bay leaf
⅜ cup red wine
1 tbsp. tomato paste
1 can (15 oz.) green lentils, drained
1 can (14½ oz.) tomatoes
2 eggplants
½ cup natural yogurt
Handful chopped parsley
Pinch of red pepper flakes

Make a big batch of the base to keep in the freezer, and if you don't like eggplant, use zucchini or beefsteak tomatoes instead.

Heat 1 tablespoon olive oil in a heavy-bottomed saucepan, then cook the onion until softened. Add the garlic, cinnamon, oregano and bay leaf, and cook until fragrant. Pour in the wine, bubble until reduced, then stir in the tomato paste, green lentils and their liquid, chopped tomatoes, and ⅜ cup water. Simmer for 30 minutes, then season.

Preheat the oven to 375°F. Meanwhile, slice the eggplants into rounds. Put on a baking sheet, drizzle with oil, turn over a few times, and season. Roast for 15 minutes, turning halfway through cooking. Spoon the yogurt into a bowl and stir through the parsley and a pinch of red pepper flakes. To serve, spoon the lentils into bowls, then top with the eggplant slices and yogurt. Serves 4.

Honey

As Winnie the Pooh, honey's highest-profile fan, says, "The only thing better than honey is more honey." Happily, it's incredibly versatile, from simply spreading on toast, to whisking into salad dressings and meat marinades, and enticing the sweetness from roast vegetables. There are, however, many different kinds to choose from—manuka, acacia, honeydew, wildflower—which not only differ in flavor, from light and floral to amber and aromatic, and texture, but also price. The lighter the color, the more subtle the flavor will be; golden, amber honeys are more caramelly with fruity notes, while the darker colors tend to be more robust.

PAIRS WITH	Sausages, ham, chicken, salmon, parsnips, butternut squash, carrots, cheese (Manchego, halloumi, feta, ricotta, goat cheese), yogurt, whisky, peaches, figs, banana, cherry, mustard, pine nuts, cinnamon, tahini, and nuts (walnuts, hazelnuts, pistachios).
HEALTH	This depends on how your honey has been processed, but the sticky stuff has long been used for its medicinal properties, including as an antiseptic, to help with hayfever (if local), and my mom's tonic (along with lemon, maybe ginger) to soothe sore throats.
HACK	Honey can be a good substitute for sugar in candies; use in bakes that should have a soft texture, ice creams, and quick breads.

Honey and rosemary roast nuts

1½ cups assorted nuts
¼ cup pumpkin seeds
1 tbsp. olive oil
2 tbsp. golden honey
1 sprig rosemary, leaves
   finely chopped
1 tsp. ground black pepper

Use any combination of nuts you like: almonds, cashews, pecans, brazils.

Preheat the oven to 400°F. Combine the nuts, pumpkin seeds, oil, honey, a large pinch of salt, and rosemary. Tip into a lined roasting pan and roast, stirring occasionally, for 12–15 minutes, until golden. Remove from the oven, stir in the black pepper, and leave to cool in the pan. Transfer to an airtight container. Serves 6.

Baked honey feta with tomatoes

7 oz. block feta
1½ tbsp. golden honey
1¾ cups cherry tomatoes,
   halved
1 tsp. chopped thyme
Pinch of pul biber
Drizzle of olive oil

There's no better way to feature feta than sat in the middle of a pile of tomatoes and baked. This works particularly well served with a green salad and crusty bread for lunch.

Preheat the oven to 400°F. Put the feta in the middle of an aluminum foil-lined baking dish and brush with the honey. Place the tomatoes around the feta, then sprinkle over the thyme, a pinch of pul biber, and season with salt and black pepper. Drizzle with oil, and bake for 30 minutes, or until the feta is softened and lightly golden. Serves 4.

Honey-mustard sausages with sweet potato

6 sausages
3 large sweet potatoes,
   cut into small chunks
2 red onions, cut into
   wedges
3 tbsp. golden honey
3 tbsp. wholegrain mustard
Drizzle of olive oil
1 tsp. chopped rosemary

Sweet from the honey with a kick from the mustard, this pan bake is a real throw-together dinner.

Preheat the oven to 400°F. Put the sausages, sweet potato, and onions in a roasting pan. In a bowl, mix the honey, mustard, a drizzle of oil, and the rosemary. Pour this over the sausages/veg, season with salt and pepper, and toss everything together. Roast for 50 minutes, until the sausages and sweet potatoes are cooked through. Serves 3.

Honey roast grape and goat cheese toast

Walnuts would make a good substitute if you don't have pecans.

Oil, for greasing
Handful red grapes
Drizzle of golden honey
Small handful thyme leaves
Toast (sourdough, for preference)
Soft goat cheese
Handful toasted pecans, crushed

Lightly oil a baking sheet then add the grapes. Drizzle with honey, scatter with thyme and a pinch of salt, and roast for 25-30 minutes, until the grapes start to burst. Spread a slice of toast with soft goat cheese, then top with the roast grapes and their juices. Sprinkle with extra thyme leaves, a handful of toasted pecans, and season with pepper. Serves 1.

Honey and pistachio cakes

These little cakes are best served warm with a spoonful of poached, tart fruit (such as rhubarb) and some sour cream.

⅔ cup unsalted butter
⅝ cup golden honey
2 eggs
¼ cup superfine sugar
1 cup all-purpose flour
1 tsp. baking powder
1 cup pistachios
1 large orange, zested

Preheat the oven to 400°F. Put the butter and honey in a saucepan and warm until the butter has melted. Meanwhile, whisk the eggs and sugar until pale, then fold in the flour and baking powder. Whizz the pistachios in a food processor until finely ground, then add to the bowl with the orange zest, a pinch of salt, and the butter/honey mix. Spoon into a lined muffin pan, then bake for about 20 minutes, until golden and a toothpick inserted into the center comes out clean. Makes 12.

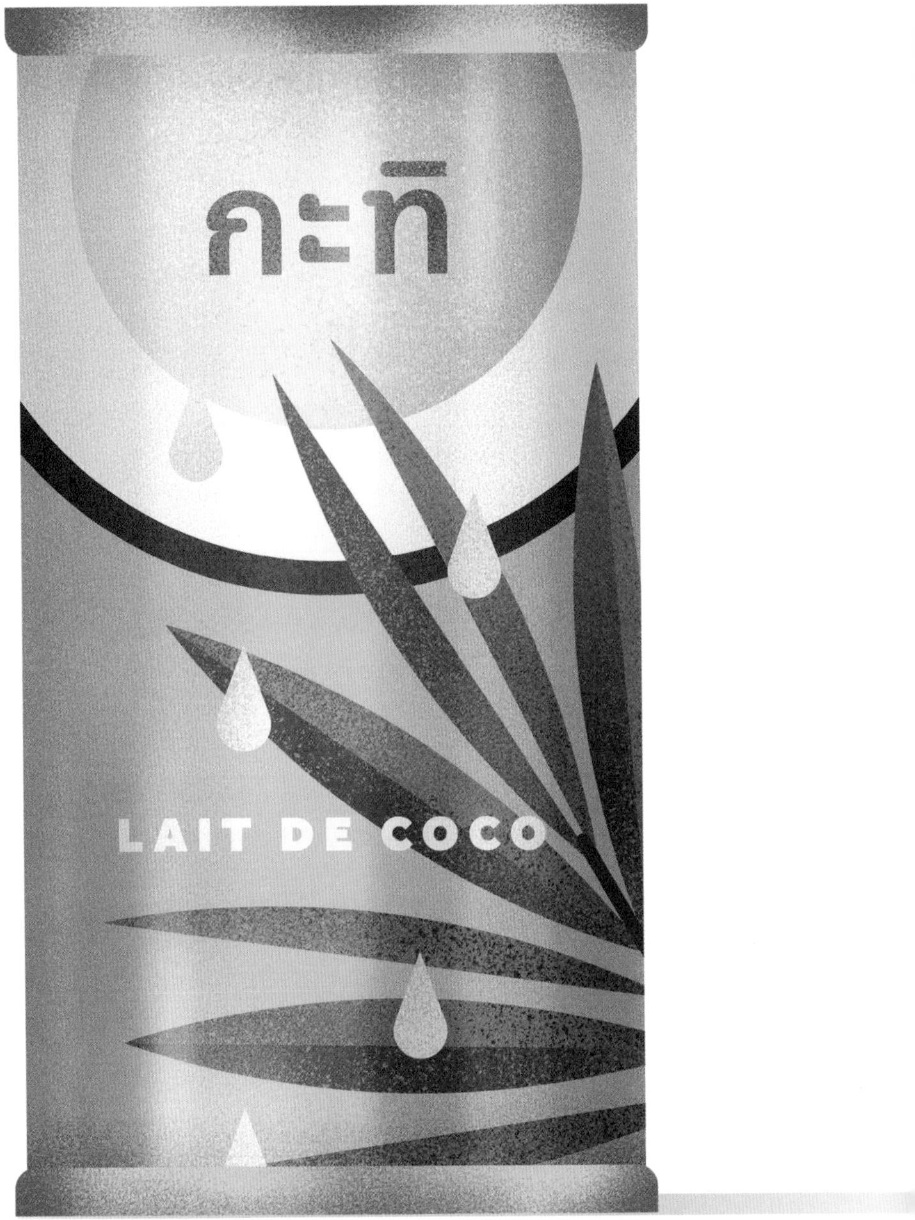

กะทิ
LAIT DE COCO

Coconut milk

Of course, you can't milk a coconut, so we're talking about shredded coconut flesh that has been pureed with water and strained. The result is a rich, white liquid that's light in consistency and naturally sweet, which will give curries, dals, soups (like tom kha), and candies depth and body. I prefer the Thai brands of coconut milk, as they tend to have a higher fat content; you'll find a solid white layer at the top of your can, which is richer in flavor, and a watery milk below, so give the can a shake before using. And always buy unsweetened.

TRANSFORM	If you are dairy free, use coconut milk in place of dairy in ice creams, loaf cakes, and rice pudding.
HEALTH	Plant-based and lactose-free, coconut milk also contains medium-chain fatty acids.
HACK	Store any leftovers in airtight containers in the refrigerator; it absorbs flavors easily so don't be tempted to keep it in the can.

Raspberry and coconut ice popsicles

1 banana
1¼ cups raspberries
1 cup coconut milk
1 tbsp. golden honey

Coconut milk is a good substitute for milk in iced desserts, like ice cream and popsicles. Use your favorite berries here - strawberries would also be good.

In a food processor, blitz the banana. Add the raspberries, blitz again, then add the coconut milk and honey and whizz for a final time. Divide between six popsicle molds and freeze overnight until solid. Makes 6.

Coconut rice

1 cup jasmine rice, rinsed
1 cup coconut milk
Handful cilantro, chopped

Subtly sweet, light, and fluffy, and a good vehicle for curries or gingery vegetables.

Put the rice in a saucepan with the coconut milk, 2¼ cups water, and a pinch of salt. Bring to a boil, stirring occasionally to prevent sticking, then turn down the heat and cook, covered, for 15 minutes until the liquid has been absorbed and the rice is cooked. Remove from the heat and leave, covered, for another 5 minutes. Fluff with a fork and scatter with the cilantro. Serves 2.

Cauliflower, carrot, and spinach dal

Coconut oil
1 garlic clove, minced
1 small red onion, finely
   chopped
¾ inch-piece ginger, minced
1 tsp. ground cilantro seeds
1 tsp. ground cumin seeds
1 tsp. ground turmeric
½ cup red lentils
1 cup coconut milk
2¼ cups vegetable broth
1 small cauliflower, cut
   into florets
1 large carrot, diced
2 handfuls spinach
Squeeze of lemon juice
Handful cilantro

Dal doesn't need a companion to be spectacular, but rice or flatbreads and salted yogurt would be no bad thing.

Heat a little coconut oil in a saucepan, add the garlic, onion, and ginger, and cook until soft, about 10 minutes. Add the cilantro seeds, cumin seeds, and turmeric, and cook for a few minutes until fragrant. Add the lentils, coconut milk, broth, cauliflower florets, and diced carrot. Bring to a simmer, then cook gently, stirring occasionally, for 30 minutes. Stir through the spinach, add a squeeze of lemon juice, and serve topped with cilantro. Serves 2.

Sweet corn and peanut curry

⅓ cup peanuts
1 tbsp. coconut oil
1 tsp. cumin seeds
1 tsp. black mustard seeds
8 curry leaves
1 tsp. turmeric
1 onion, diced
2 garlic cloves, diced
1-in. piece ginger, chopped
Half a green chile, chopped
1 can (14½ oz.) tomatoes
1 cup coconut milk
2 ears of corn, kernels
    removed (or 21/4 cups
    frozen sweet corn)
Half a lemon, juiced
½ cup cilantro, chopped

I love a Gujurati peanut and sweet corn curry served with a load of chapatis. And this is my version.

Dry roast the peanuts in a hot pan until golden, then crush in a mortar. In the same pan, heat the coconut oil then add the cumin seeds, black mustard seeds, and, once they start to pop, stir in the curry leaves and turmeric. Cook for 30 seconds, then add the onion, cook until softened, then add the garlic, ginger, and green chile. Continue cooking for a minute, then add the chopped tomatoes, coconut milk, and a splash of water, and simmer for 8 minutes. Add the sweet corn and most of the peanuts, cover, and cook for 15 minutes. Add the lemon juice and cilantro, and serve topped with the reserved peanuts. Serves 3-4.

Sweet potato, coconut, and lime soup

Peanut oil
3 scallions, chopped
1 thumb-size piece of
    ginger, minced
1 red chile, chopped
1 lemongrass, outer leaves
    removed, stalk finely
    chopped
4 sweet potatoes, peeled
    and diced
4 cups broth
1 cup coconut milk
1 lime, zested and juiced
Handful cilantro

Creamy, sweet, and spicy, this makes for a really comforting bowl.

Heat a splash of peanut oil in a heavy-bottomed saucepan. Fry the scallions, ginger, chile, and lemongrass. Once softened, add the diced sweet potato, give everything a good stir, then pour in the broth and coconut milk. Bring to a boil, cover, and simmer for 20 minutes, until the potatoes are cooked. Blend until smooth. Stir through the lime zest and juice, and finish with cilantro. Serves 6.

Preserved lemons

A jar of this fragrant, slightly tart fruit will brighten and add depth to dressings, salsas, dips, and sauces; oily fish; salads; stews and grilled meat. Commonly associated with North African cooking, the process is simple: take unwaxed lemons, cut lengthwise into quarters (leaving the base attached), then stuff with coarse sea salt. These go into a sterilized jar and you can then either leave them neat or add herbs or spices. Once softened (which takes at least a month), they can be used by either blending the rind and pulp (pips removed) into a paste (to go into sauces, marinades, vinaigrettes) or slicing or mincing the rind for stews, curries, and pan bakes or stirring through grains. Whichever way, give the lemons a rinse first to remove the brine.

PAIR WITH	Oily fish, seafood, grilled meat, vegetables (cauliflower, potatoes, peas, zucchini, kale), couscous, butter beans, spelt, barley, rice, lentils, ricotta, and yogurt.
TRANSFORM	Add a burst of flavor to your Sunday lunch by stuffing into a chicken before roasting; basting the bird with the lemon juices; or blitz, then combine with olive oil and some seasoning, and pour over roast meat.
HACK	When life gives you too many preserved lemons, remove the pips, blitz the rind and flesh, and decant into ice-cube trays.

Lemon and green olive spaghetti

7 oz. spaghetti
¼ cup olive oil
2 garlic cloves, sliced
Pinch of red pepper flakes
Rind of 2 preserved lemons, chopped
⅔ cup pitted green olives, roughly chopped
⅔ cup Parmesan, grated
Squeeze of lemon juice
Handful basil leaves

Consider this a vote for a simpler meal. A good squeeze of fresh lemon juice and a handful of basil leaves keep this pantry dinner feeling fresh.

Cook the spaghetti in salted boiling water according to the package instructions until al dente. Meanwhile, heat the oil in a saucepan over medium heat. Add the garlic and red pepper flakes, then fry for 30 seconds. Add the chopped preserved lemon skin and green olives, and cook for another minute or so. Using tongs, add the cooked pasta to the preserved lemon mix, adding a splash of pasta cooking water, then take off the heat. Add the Parmesan, a good squeeze of fresh lemon juice, and black pepper to taste. Add torn basil leaves, toss again, and serve with extra basil and Parmesan. Serves 2.

Preserved lemon vinaigrette

2 tbsp. white wine vinegar
6 tbsp. extra virgin olive oil
1 preserved lemon, rind finely chopped
2 tsp. Dijon mustard

Everyone needs a good vinaigrette in their arsenal, and even the simplest adjustment can keep things interesting. Here, that's the addition of preserved lemon.

Put the vinegar, olive oil, the preserved lemon rind, and Dijon mustard in a jar. Season, put the lid on, and shake well to mix.

Preserved lemonade

1 preserved lemon
2 tbsp. fresh lemon juice
Small handful mint leaves
2 tbsp. sugar
Ice
Soda or tonic water

Preserved and fresh lemons are combined for a taste of summer days.

Halve the preserved lemon, remove the pips, then blitz the flesh and rind in a food processor with the fresh lemon juice, mint leaves, and sugar. Put ice into two glasses, pour over half the lemon mix into each, and top up with soda or tonic water. Serves 2.

Preserved lemon drizzle cake

2 preserved lemons
½ cup + 1 tbsp. unsalted butter, softened
½ cup + 2 tbsp. superfine sugar
2 eggs
2 lemons, juiced
1 cup all-purpose flour
1 tsp. baking powder

FOR THE SYRUP
½ cup superfine sugar
2 lemons, juiced

Harness the savory side of preserved lemons and give the humble lemon drizzle a fragrant kick. A good example of minimal effort, maximum results.

Preheat the oven to 375°F and grease a 1lb. loaf pan. Whizz the rind of the preserved lemons in a food processor until fine. In a bowl, beat the butter and sugar until light and fluffy. Add the eggs, beating well between each addition, followed by the whizzed preserved lemon, lemon juice, flour, baking powder, and a pinch of salt. Spoon the mixture into the pan and bake for 35-40 minutes, until lightly golden and a toothpick inserted into the center comes out clean.

Run a knife around the edge of the pan and prick the cake all over with a toothpick. To make the syrup, heat the sugar and lemon juice in a saucepan until the sugar dissolves. Pour the syrup over the warm cake and set aside to cool in the pan. Serves 10-12.

Preserved lemon hasselback potatoes

1¾ lb. floury potatoes
3½ tbsp. olive oil
3 preserved lemons
1 tbsp. chopped thyme

Golden, crisp, and fragrant from the preserved lemon, these hasselbacks are a fine alternative Sunday roast side dish. Using similar-size potatoes will help them cook evenly.

Preheat the oven to 400°F. Carefully make vertical slits, about ⅛ inch apart, three-quarters of the way down and all the way along the potatoes. In a bowl, combine the olive oil, finely chopped rind of the preserved lemons, and thyme, and season generously. Add the potatoes to the bowl and coat them in the oil. Transfer to a roasting dish cut-side up, drizzling any remaining oil on the potatoes, and roast for 1 hour, spooning the oil over occasionally, until golden and tender. Serves 3-4.

Nuts and seeds

Whether you're in need of something crunchy, creamy, sweet or spicy, nuts and seeds have you covered; a handful of almonds, hazelnuts, walnuts, pumpkin, or sesame seeds will bring texture, flavor, and nutrients to everything they touch. Cashews, when blended, are a good substitute for cream or milk; walnuts and hazelnuts have a rightful place in pesto; roasted, nuts and seeds make a great snack or topper for salads and pan bakes; ground almonds or pecans bring depth of flavor to cakes; while a handful of mixed seeds can bring a welcome crunch when kneaded into a basic bread dough. They really are a secret weapon.

TRANSFORM	Cashew cream brings richness and body to dairy-free pastas, soups, or overnight oats. Soak the nuts in boiling water for half an hour, before draining and blending with fresh water until completely smooth.
HEALTH	High in unsaturated fat, with polyphenols supporting gut health, nuts also contain protein, fiber, minerals, such as iron and magnesium, B and E vitamins. Walnuts, chia, flax, and hemp are plant-based sources of omega-3 fats.
HACK	Make your own nut butter by roasting peanuts, cashews, or almonds (or a mixture), then blending in a food processor until smooth and creamy—be patient, it will take a while. And don't forget to add a little salt.

Pumpkin seed butter

3 cups pumpkin seeds
1 tbsp. golden honey

**My favorite way to eat this is on toast
with a drizzle of golden honey.**

Preheat the oven to 325°F. Put the pumpkin seeds on a lined cookie
sheet and roast for 15 minutes. Tip the seeds into a food processor
and blitz, scraping down the sides occasionally, for 10-15 minutes
until smooth. Add the honey and a pinch of salt and blitz again
very briefly. This will keep at room temperature for up to a week.
Makes 3 cups.

Cashew and date energy balls

⅓ cup cashews
1½ cups Medjool dates,
   chopped
¼ cup flaked coconut

**These will keep in an airtight container
in the refrigerator for five days.**

Blitz the cashews, dates, flaked coconut, and a pinch of salt in
a food processor until a dough forms. Roll into eight balls then
refrigerate, covered, in the refrigerator for 1 hour. Makes 8.

Tahini granola

1¼ cups mixed nuts,
   chopped
1 tbsp. sesame seeds
1 cup rolled oats
2 tsp. cinnamon
¼ tsp. salt
¼ cup maple syrup
2 tbsp. olive oil
3 tbsp. tahini

**This is heavy on the nuts; use a mix of whatever you fancy,
but I like almonds, walnuts, and pistachios.**

Preheat the oven to 325°F. In a bowl, combine the nuts, sesame
seeds, oats, cinnamon, and salt. Add the maple syrup, olive oil, and
tahini. Give everything a good mix, then spoon onto a lined baking
sheet. Bake at for 40 minutes, stirring halfway through cooking,
until golden. Cool completely before eating. Serves 6-8.

Leek, sage, and walnut tart

3–4 tbsp. olive oil
5 leeks, thinly sliced
15 sage leaves, sliced
Half a lemon, zested and juiced
12 oz. puff pastry sheet
1 cup soft goat cheese
Large handful walnuts, broken up

I like to use a round puff pastry sheet here, but a rectangular one will work just as well.

Heat 3 tablespoons olive oil in a heavy-bottomed saucepan, then cook the leeks, sage leaves, and a pinch of salt for 15 minutes, until the leeks are really soft. Stir in the lemon zest and juice, season with black pepper, then remove from the heat.

Preheat the oven to 400°F. Unroll a sheet of puff pastry on a baking sheet and mark a ¾-inch border. Bake for 20 minutes, until puffed up and golden. Remove from the oven and push the middle down with the back of a spoon. Tip over the leek mixture, then crumble over the goat cheese, followed by the walnuts, a little black pepper, and a drizzle of oil. Bake again for 10 minutes until golden. Serves 6.

Hazelnut pesto

¾ cup hazelnuts
1⅓ cups flat-leaf parsley
1 lemon, zested and juiced
1 garlic clove, crushed
½ cup Parmesan, grated
2–3 tbsp. olive oil

The easiest way to remove the skins from the toasted hazelnuts is to roll them between kitchen towel—it doesn't matter if they don't all come off, you won't notice it in the final sauce.

Toast the hazelnuts in a dry skillet until fragrant, then leave to cool a little before removing the skins. Transfer the nuts to a food processor with the parsley (or a mix of parsley and basil), the lemon zest and juice, garlic, and Parmesan. Blitz to a paste then, with the motor still running, drizzle in the olive oil until you've got a creamy consistency. Season to taste. Serves 6-8.

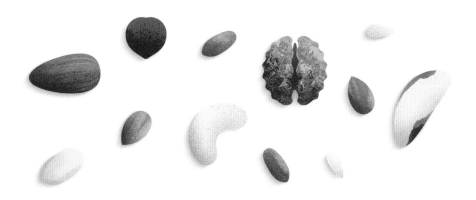

Preserved cherries

Cherry season is short, so other than baking them in a pie you're probably better off enjoying the jewellike fruit straight from the bag or served cold over ice. Canned dark sweet cherries, however, are ripe for baking or incorporating into desserts all year round. Also sold in jars, the cherries are stored in a light sugar syrup or kirsch, which can be drained off before adding the fruit to brownies, crumbles or sponges. I find cherries in syrup to be more versatile; the syrup can be simmered with the fruit and spooned over ice cream or yogurt, or used to brush the sponge of a Black Forest gateau before frosting.

PAIR WITH	Chocolate, coconut, berries, almond, pistachio, yogurt, ricotta, rum, and herbs (basil, rosemary, thyme).
TRANSFORM	A can of cherries will give you an instant sauce, ideal for topping pancakes. Heat the contents of the can with some cornstarch, stirring constantly until syrupy, then set aside. Keep things interesting by playing around with different spices.
HACK	Save the drained syrup and use to soak your overnight oats.

Cherry and basil friands

Herbs can bring a new dimension to old favorites. Here, the basil adds a floral note to the classic friand.

¼ cup + 3 tbsp. unsalted butter, plus extra for greasing
3 tbsp. all-purpose flour
1 cup confectioners' sugar
¾ cup + 2 tbsp. ground almonds
1 lemon, zested
3 egg whites
½ cup canned dark sweet cherries, plus 3 to decorate, halved
Small handful basil, shredded

Preheat the oven to 350°F. Grease and line six holes of a muffin or friand pan with paper baking cups. In a small saucepan, heat the butter until it starts to brown; cool slightly. In a large bowl, stir together the flour and confectioners' sugar, then add the ground almonds and lemon zest. In another bowl, beat the egg whites until you have a soft foam, then tip into the flour mix along with the melted butter. Stir in the cherries and basil, then pour into the paper baking cups and top each cake with a cherry half. Bake for 30 minutes, until golden. Leave to cool for 10 minutes in the pan, then transfer to a wire rack to cool completely. Makes 6.

Cherry and rosemary shrub

Shrubs combine fruit and vinegar for a puckering but refreshing nonalcoholic drink.

¼ cup canned dark sweet cherries, drained and liquid reserved
2 tbsp. white wine vinegar
2 sprigs rosemary leaves, finely chopped
Soda water

Finely chop the cherries and add to a bowl with ½ cup of their liquid, the vinegar and rosemary. Set aside for at least 1 hour. Taste and adjust as needed. Pour ¼ cup over ice into two glasses, then top up with soda water. Serves 2.

Cherry and coconut crumble

The real magic of a crumble lies in that squidgy layer between the filling and topping, which is achieved by having plenty of fruit and enough crumble to soak it up.

¼ cup unsalted butter, cubed
¾ cup + 1 tsp. all-purpose flour
⅓ cup light brown sugar, packed
½ cup rolled oats
⅔ cup flaked coconut
1 can (15 oz.) dark sweet cherries, drained
1 lemon, zest of half then juiced

Preheat the oven to 400°F. In a bowl, rub the butter and flour together, then stir through the sugar, oats, and coconut. Tip the cherries into an ovenproof dish, then add the lemon zest and juice, plus ¼ cup water. Tip over the crumble mix, then bake for 20-25 minutes until bubbling. Serves 6.

Quick-pickled cherries

1 cup canned dark sweet cherries, drained and liquid reserved

2 tsp. cider vinegar

1 tsp. superfine sugar

½ tsp. cilantro seeds, crushed

Pinch of red pepper flakes

While canned cherries are often used in sweet scenarios, once pickled they bring a welcome burst of flavor to zucchini or beet salads.

Chop the cherries and combine in a bowl with the vinegar, sugar, cilantro seeds, red pepper flakes, and 1 tablespoon of the canned cherry liquid. Set aside for 30 minutes. Makes 1 jar.

Cherry and ricotta cake

⅔ cup unsalted butter, softened

¾ cup + 2 tbsp. light brown sugar, packed

1 tsp. vanilla bean paste

1 lemon, zested

3 eggs

1⅓ cups + 2 tbsp. all-purpose flour

2 tsp. baking powder

½ tsp. salt

1 cup ricotta

1 ½ cups canned dark sweet cherries, drained

A simple sponge made nice and squidgy by the addition of ricotta.

Line an 8-inch round cake pan with parchment paper. In a large bowl, beat the butter, sugar, vanilla paste, and the lemon zest until pale and fluffy. Add the eggs one at a time, beating well between each addition.

Preheat the oven to 375°F. In another bowl, combine the flour, baking powder, and salt, then tip into the batter and combine. Stir in the ricotta, then spoon into the prepared pan. Push the cherries into the batter, then bake for 1 hour, or until firm to the touch and a toothpick inserted into the center comes out clean—cover with aluminum foil if the top starts browning too much. Leave to cool completely before serving. Serves 8-10.

Peanut butter

Peanut butter holds so much potential: if you're in need of something sweet, it's there; if your craving is altogether saltier, you're also covered. While often all that's required is to pile it onto toast or into celery, peanut butter is also the force behind quick, simple noodle sauces and dressings, shortcuts to curries, and West African-inspired stews. Sweet salve, meanwhile, can be found in cheesecakes, pancakes, and frosting. That said, not all peanut butter is created the same; different jars contain different quantities of salt and sugar (or other sweeteners), while others might add flavorings, such as vanilla or cocoa.

VARIETIES	Smooth and crunchy are the main players, and they're mostly interchangeable. You then have the all-natural, organic, chocolate (or other flavorings) ones to contend with and there's also the roast—long roast times lead to a stronger color and flavor, while raw or blanched peanuts mean a lighter, creamier result.
HEALTH	A good source of plant protein, healthy fats, and minerals (magnesium, iron, zinc) and vitamins (B and E). Be aware that many brands add sugar, salt, oil, and emulsifiers.
HACK	Making your own is no hardship; all you're doing is roasting blanched peanuts then, once cool, blending in a food processor. Add oil (peanut), whizz again, then add salt, golden honey, or whatever you fancy.

Sweet potato, peanut, and spinach stew

1 tbsp. coconut oil

1 onion, roughly chopped

2 garlic cloves, finely chopped

Thumb-size piece of ginger, finely grated

1 red bell pepper, roughly chopped

1 green bell pepper, roughly chopped

2 tsp. cilantro seeds

1 tsp. cumin seeds

2 tbsp. peanut butter

2½ cups vegetable broth

4 small sweet potatoes, peeled and chopped into bite-size chunks

Handful spinach

This rich sauce makes a good base for using up whatever vegetables you have to hand. That said, roots and greens work best.

Heat the oil in a saucepan over medium heat, then add the onion, garlic, ginger, and the red and green bell peppers, until softened—about 10 minutes. Grind the cilantro seeds and cumin seeds in a mortar then add to the pan, cooking for 1-2 minutes.

Stir in the peanut butter and vegetable broth, then add the sweet potatoes. Cover and cook for half an hour, until the potatoes are cooked through. Add the spinach, stirring to wilt, then season and serve with rice. Serves 3.

Peanut butter crispy bars

¾ cup + 1 tbsp. dark chocolate chips

¼ cup + 2½ tbsp. smooth peanut butter

½ tsp. vanilla extract

4 tbsp. golden honey

5½ cups puffed rice

FOR THE TOPPING

¼ cup dark chocolate chips

Handful roasted peanuts, chopped

A slightly more grown-up version of the classic rice crispy cake. Be sure the mix is fully set before slicing.

Melt the dark chocolate, peanut butter, vanilla extract, and honey in a bowl over (but not touching) a saucepan of simmering water, stirring until smooth. Remove the bowl from the heat then stir through the puffed rice until coated completely.

Spoon into a square pan lined with parchment paper (or paper baking cups), then refrigerate until set—about 2 hours. Melt the remaining chocolate, drizzle over the set crispy cake, and decorate with chopped peanuts. Slice into bars. Makes 12-14.

Spicy peanut sauce

¼ cup + 2½ tbsp. peanut butter

1 garlic clove, minced

2 tbsp. kecap manis

½ tsp. crushed Sichuan peppercorns

1 lime, juiced

Pinch of flaky sea salt

This is highly customizable, so play around adding chili oil or sriracha, then eat with grilled meats, noodles, salads, dumplings, and summer rolls.

In a bowl, whisk together the peanut butter, minced garlic, kecap manis, Sichuan pepper, lime juice, sea salt, and a splash of boiling water. Serves 2.

Peanut noodles with smacked cucumber

2 tsp. sesame oil
1 tbsp. golden honey
3 tbsp. peanut butter
3 tbsp. soy sauce
3 tbsp. rice vinegar
1 thumb-size piece of grated ginger
2 garlic cloves, grated
1 medium-size cucumber
7 oz. rice noodles
Handful cilantro leaves
Roasted peanuts, chopped, to serve
Scallions, sliced, to serve

The crunch from the cucumber adds freshness, while "smacking" them means they'll soak up the sauce better.

In a bowl, combine the sesame oil, honey, peanut butter, soy sauce, rice vinegar, ginger, and garlic.

Use a rolling pin to bash the cucumber on a board until it breaks apart. Chop into chunks, put in a bowl, sprinkle with salt, and set aside. Cook the rice noodles according to the package instructions, then drain, rinse under cold water, and return to the pan. Mix in the sauce and cucumber, and serve with the cilantro, chopped roasted peanuts, and sliced scallions. Serves 2.

PBJ yogurt parfait

1½ cups strawberries
1 tbsp. sugar
Squeeze of lime juice
1 cinnamon stick
½ cup natural yogurt
2 tbsp. peanut butter
Handful granola

Peanut butter and jelly is the ultimate union of sweet and salty. For this breakfast parfait, I've swapped the jelly for strawberries roasted with lime and cinnamon, but other berries would work well, too.

Preheat the oven to 425°F. Hull and halve the strawberries then transfer to an ovenproof dish and toss with the sugar, lime juice, and cinnamon stick. Bake for 15-20 minutes, until softened, then leave to cool, discarding the cinnamon stick.

To serve, spoon a quarter of the yogurt into two bowls and top each one with ½ tablespoon peanut butter, followed by some of the cooked strawberries and a sprinkling of granola. Repeat the layers. Serves 2.

Kimchi

Eaten from the jar, this fermented Korean condiment is crunchy, sour, and funky, but once heat is applied, kimchi mellows and its sweetness emerges. For this reason, it is wonderful to cook with, adding a savory kick when stirred into the likes of fried rice, stews, omelets, or even spaghetti. Although kimchi is commonly made with napa cabbage and daikon, there are many varieties to choose from, such as the fire-red baechu, or a more subtle radish water ferment called dongchimi. And if you're making it yourself, experiment by mixing up the vegetables, from daikon and kohlrabi to different greens.

PAIRS WITH	Chicken, pork, beef, shrimp, tofu, Cheddar, Parmesan, sweet potato, potato, cauliflower, carrot, mushroom, sweet corn, tomato, ginger, scallion, egg, and gochujang.
HEALTH	Kimchi contains probiotics and good bacteria, which supports the gut.
HACK	Kimchi varies in quality and saltiness, so taste and adjust the seasoning to suit you.

Creamy kimchi udon

7 oz. udon noodles
¾ cup frozen sweet corn
1 tbsp. oil
1 large white onion, sliced
½ cup kimchi, chopped
½ cup shredded Cheddar
2 scallions, sliced

Kimchi and Cheddar are the perfect match, especially when used to coat udon noodles.

Cook the noodles according to the package instructions, adding the sweet corn in the last few minutes. In a large saucepan, heat the oil, then add the onion and a pinch of salt, and cook until caramelized. Add the kimchi, cook for a couple of minutes, then add the cooked noodles, sweet corn, cheese, and a splash of the noodle cooking water. Give everything a good mix, then season with black pepper and top with the scallions. Serves 2.

Baked kimchi and kale rice with eggs

⅔ cup jasmine rice
1–2 tsp. toasted
    sesame oil
2 tbsp. soy sauce
1 cup chopped kale
½ cup kimchi, chopped
4 eggs
Sesame seeds, to serve
Scallions, sliced,
    to serve

A hands-off approach to fluffy rice, which is greater than the sum of its parts.

Preheat the oven to 425°F. Put the rice in an ovenproof pan with 1 teaspoon sesame oil, the soy sauce, ¾ cup water, and a pinch of salt, and combine. Bring to a simmer, then turn down the heat and cook for 12 minutes. Stir through the kale and kimchi, then cover and bake for 5 minutes. Give everything a stir, then make four holes in the rice. Crack in the eggs, cover, and return to the oven for 7 minutes, until the egg whites are set. Serve drizzled with a little sesame oil, a scattering of sesame seeds, and scallions. Serves 2.

Kimchi pancakes

2½ tbsp. all-purpose flour
2 tbsp. rice flour
½ tsp. baking powder
¼ cup cold water
1 tbsp. kimchi juice
½–1 tsp. gochujang
    (depending on spice
    preference)
¾ cup kimchi, chopped
2 scallions, chopped
Splash of oil

You could make this as one large pancake, or two smaller ones.

Combine the flours and baking powder in a bowl, then whisk in the cold water, the kimchi liquid, and gochujang. Mix in the kimchi and scallions. Heat a splash of oil in a nonstick skillet, then add the batter. Cook for a few minutes until the bottom is golden brown and bubbles appear on the surface, then flip and continue cooking on the other side for 2 minutes, until golden. Serves 2.

Kimchi and grilled cheese

⅜ cup shredded Cheddar
⅜ cup shredded Emmental
2 scallions, sliced
4 slices sourdough
¾ cup kimchi, drained
Butter

Grilled cheese sandwiches always benefit from ferments or a bit of heat—and here you get both.

Combine the cheeses and scallions in a bowl. Divide a third of the mixture between two slices of bread and top each one with kimchi. Sprinkle over the remaining cheese, top each one with a slice of bread, and butter all sides. Heat a large skillet, add the sandwiches, and cook for 5 minutes, pressing down firmly with a spatula. Flip and cook for another 3 minutes. Serves 2.

Kimchi bubble and squeak

14 oz. floury potatoes, halved
1 tbsp. olive oil
1 large white onion, chopped
¾ cup kimchi, chopped
Handful cilantro leaves, chopped

Don't worry if the bubble breaks upon flipping, just pat it back together with a spatula.

Simmer the potatoes in salted boiling water until soft, about 15 minutes. Drain, then roughly mash with a fork. Meanwhile, heat the oil in a large skillet. Add the onion and cook until soft, about 10 minutes. Add the kimchi, cook for 2 minutes, then add the potatoes and cilantro, then season with salt and pepper. Push the mix into the base of the pan with a spatula and cook for 6 minutes until the bottom is golden. Flip and continue cooking for 4 minutes. Serves 2-3.

Anchovies

Small but mighty, the salty, umami flavor of anchovies means a little really does go a long way. While this oil-packed fish can be used straight from the jar, remember the oil is precious too, so add it wherever you're using the fish, or when roasting vegetables or in pasta sauces. Puttanesca, Caesar salad, bread crumbs, or as a topper for pizza or an onion tart are all eminently sensible ways to use up stray fillets, and when it comes to those broken-up bits lurking in the bottom of the can, deploy them in mayonnaise or vinaigrettes—the salty hit is ideal for grain salads. Be sure to submerge any leftover anchovies in oil and store in an airtight container in the refrigerator.

PAIR WITH	Steak, sea bass, cod, hake, broccoli, potato, asparagus, tomato, kale, globe artichoke, fennel, red pepper, radish, chicory, chile, ricotta, Parmesan, lemon, sage, capers, eggs, cannellini beans, and tahini.
TRANSFORM	For a take on pan con tomate, smear any broken bits of anchovy and their oil on grilled focaccia, and top with tomato.
HACK	Combine finely chopped anchovies (plus garlic, lemon juice, and some seasoning) with softened unsalted butter and use to rub on roast chicken.

Broccoli and anchovy gratin

3–4 tbsp. olive oil
2 white onions, sliced
2 garlic cloves, chopped
1 red chile, chopped
5 anchovies in oil
2 large heads broccoli, florets and stalks chopped into bite-size pieces
½ cup dry bread crumbs
1 lemon, zested
⅓ cup Parmesan, grated

Few things cosset and hug quite like a gratin, and this green version would be happy as a side or main.

Heat 3 tablespoons oil in an ovenproof pan, then cook the onions with some salt and pepper until very soft—about 15 minutes. Add the garlic, chile, and anchovies, and cook, stirring occasionally, while you get on with the broccoli. Tip the florets and stalks into a saucepan of boiling water and blanch for 3 minutes. Drain, refresh under cold water, and tip into the onion pan. Season generously with black pepper.

Preheat the oven to 400°F. In a small bowl, combine the bread crumbs, lemon zest, and Parmesan. Tip over the gratin, drizzle with oil, and bake for 20 minutes, until golden. Leave for 5 minutes before serving. Serves 2.

Roast tomatoes and anchovies

2 cups cherry tomatoes, halved
3 anchovies, roughly chopped
2 garlic cloves, sliced
5 sage leaves, torn
Drizzle of olive oil

The anchovies really enhance the flavor of the tomatoes. It's a great accompaniment to white fish.

Preheat the oven to 350°F. Put the tomatoes, anchovies, garlic, sage, and some seasoning in an ovenproof dish. Drizzle with oil and roast for 40 minutes. Serves 2.

Brussels sprout and anchovy tart

2 tbsp. olive oil
1⅓ oz. anchovies, roughly chopped
3⅓ cups Brussels sprouts, shredded
1 lemon, zested and juiced
1 garlic clove, sliced
¼ cup picked thyme
12 oz. sheet puff pastry
Red onion chutney
Handful walnuts, chopped

This is a cinch to make but packs such a punch. Eat with a crisp, green salad.

Add the oil to a saucepan, then cook the anchovies until they've melted, about 3 minutes. Add the sprouts, cook for 2 minutes, then add the lemon juice and zest, garlic, and thyme, and continue cooking for a few minutes.

Preheat the oven to 425°F. Unroll the pastry onto a lined cookie sheet and score a ¼-inch border around the edge. Spread the base with red onion chutney, then tip over the sprouts. Sprinkle over the walnuts, then bake for 20 minutes, until the pastry is puffed up and golden. Let cool for 5 minutes before slicing. Serves 4.

Anchovy and lemon salsa

1 large handful flat-leaf
  parsley
1 large handful basil
4 anchovies in oil, drained
1 tbsp. capers, drained and
  rinsed
1 small garlic clove, grated
1 lemon, zested and juiced
Olive oil

Salsas are so useful and play well with many things, from white fish to bean salads.

Chop the herbs, anchovies, and capers, then transfer to a bowl. Stir in the garlic, lemon zest, and juice, followed by enough olive oil to get your preferred consistency—about 1 tablespoon. Season with salt and pepper. Serves 4.

Gildas

6 pickled Guindillas peppers
6 oil-packed anchovy fillets
  (ideally, white)
6 pitted large, green olives
  (like Manzanilla)

This is less a recipe but more of a reminder that salty, spicy gildas are a very good friend of the spritz. As with all simple snacks, though, success hinges on the quality of your ingredients.

Fold a pepper in half then skewer onto a toothpick. Next, fold an anchovy fillet in half and thread onto the stick, then finish with an olive. Repeat with the remaining peppers, anchovies, and olives. Makes 6.

Noodles

Salvation can always be found in noodles, whether it's breakfast, lunch, or dinner. That satisfying slurp from a bowl of ramen, the lightly numbing effect of sesame chili rice noodles, or a fresh soba salad better served cold than hot, with tons of lime, ginger, and cilantro. Such versatility is made possible by the sheer number of shapes and sizes noodles come in, from thick, thin, flat, and round, to springy, chewy, and delicate, with some made from wheat or rice, and others egg and pulses.

VARIETIES	Ramen, the thin, wheat noodles, are best served in broths; thicker, chewier udon can be eaten hot or cold; soba, made from buckwheat, are ideal for salads or in broths; rice noodles welcome bolder flavors and are wonderfully versatile; glass noodles are great in stir-fries or soups.
TRANSFORM	Pep up pot noodles by crowning with quick pickled, soy-coated eggs and a drizzle of chili sauce.
HACK	A good bowl of noodles relies on a sauce with tons of flavor, something textural (e.g., crunchy), and something fresh and fragrant (think herbs and citrus).

Noodles in ginger and turmeric broth with Swiss chard

Drizzle of sesame oil

1 thumb-size piece ginger, sliced

1 thumb-size piece turmeric, sliced

Half a red chile, finely chopped

2 garlic cloves, finely chopped

2¾ cups Swiss chard, stalks chopped and leaves sliced

2 cups broth

7 oz. egg noodles

Squeeze of lime juice

Splash of soy sauce

A restorative broth that is adaptable: increase the amount of ginger if you prefer; swap the egg noodles for soba, rice or udon; and season to taste with lime juice and soy sauce.

Heat a little oil in a medium saucepan, add the ginger, turmeric, red chile, garlic, and chard stalks, and cook for 2 minutes. Add the broth, bring to a simmer, then turn down the heat and gently bubble away for 15 minutes. Meanwhile, cook the noodles according to the package instructions. Drain, then divide between two bowls. Add the chard leaves to the broth, followed by a squeeze of lime and a splash of soy sauce. Taste and adjust as necessary. Ladle the broth over the noodles. Serves 2.

Crab and mango rice noodles

8 oz. rice vermicelli noodles

1 large mango, diced

¾ cup white crab meat

1 large handful Thai basil, chopped

1 large handful mint, chopped

2 tbsp. fish sauce

2 tsp. rice vinegar

3 tbsp. lime juice, plus 1 tsp. zest

Sugar

Handful roasted peanuts, chopped

1 red chile, chopped

The sweetness of crab pairs well with punchy flavors, such as chile, soy, and lime. You could also add some avocado here.

Cook the noodles according to the package instructions, then drain and rinse under water. Transfer to a bowl, then toss through the mango, crab, and most of the herbs. In a small bowl, combine the fish sauce, vinegar, lime juice, and zest with a pinch of sugar. Tip over the noodles and toss. Scatter over the peanuts, chile, and remaining herbs, and serve with lime wedges, if you like. Serves 4.

Udon carbonara

2 egg yolks
⅔ cup Parmesan, grated
½ cup pancetta, diced
Drizzle of olive oil
2 shallots, sliced
7 oz. udon noodles
2 garlic cloves, thinly sliced

Smooth, salty, and comforting, this carbonara brings together the flavors of Italy and Japan.

Whisk the egg yolks, Parmesan, and a good grind of black pepper in a bowl; set aside. In a saucepan, fry the pancetta in a little oil until crisp, then transfer to a plate. Fry the shallots in the pancetta pan until softened and beginning to brown. Meanwhile, cook the noodles according to the package instructions, then drain, reserving some cooking water. Add the garlic to the shallots, cook for 2 minutes, then stir in the noodles and pancetta. Add a splash of water to the egg mix, then tip it into the pan, tossing everything together until the sauce is thick and glossy—you may need to add a little more cooking water. Season with more black pepper. Serves 2.

Soba noodle salad

7 oz. soba noodles
¾ cup frozen edamame
2 tbsp. soy sauce
1 lime, juiced
2 tsp. miso
1 tbsp. mirin
1 thumb-size piece ginger, grated
Drizzle of sesame oil
1 handful spinach, sliced
1 large carrot, cut into matchsticks
4 scallions, sliced
Handful sesame seeds
A few nori sheets, torn

A salad to serve hot or cold, making it ideal for weekday lunches.

Cook the noodles according to the package instructions, adding the edamame in the last 2 minutes. Meanwhile, in a large bowl, whisk together the soy sauce, lime juice, miso, mirin, and ginger. When the noodles and edamame are cooked, drain and rinse under cold water. Transfer to the bowl, and drizzle with sesame oil. Add the spinach, carrot, scallions, and a handful of sesame seeds, and give everything a good mix. Serve topped with the nori. Serves 2.

Ramen pancake

4 oz, ramen noodles
1 tbsp. soy sauce
2 tsp. rice vinegar
1 tbsp. toasted sesame oil
1 red chile, finely chopped
1 thumb-size piece ginger, minced
1 large garlic clove, minced
1 tbsp. sesame seeds
1 large handful cilantro leaves, chopped
Kewpie or sriracha, to serve

The easiest way to flip this is by placing a plate over the pan, flipping and sliding the pancake back in.

Soak the noodles in boiling water for 10 minutes, then drain thoroughly. Transfer to a bowl, toss to loosen, add the remaining ingredients and toss again. Put a large skillet over medium heat, then, once hot, tip in the noodles and flatten. Cook for 7 minutes, until the bottom is golden, then flip and cook on the other side for 5 minutes. Serve squirted with kewpie or sriracha and more cilantro, if you like. Serves 2-3.

Mayonnaise

Sure, homemade mayonnaise is great—made by whisking together egg yolks, oil, garlic, salt, and vinegar or lemon juice—but I've got a lot of time for the ready-made stuff. Use neat and deploy in sandwiches, spoon over eggs, or use for dunking fries. Mayonnaise is also your shortcut to salad dressings (think Caesar) or perking up with garlic, gherkins, herbs, or, if you really want to push the boat out, saffron. It's also eminently sensible to get acquainted with kewpie, the Japanese mayo, which is smoother, richer, and has a more eggy, umami flavor—ideal for squirting over karokke (croquettes made with mashed potato and veg) or okonomiyaki (a Japanese savory pancake).

PAIR WITH	Crab, tuna, shrimp, anchovies, sardines, chicken, turkey, eggs, kale, cabbage, spinach, artichoke, sweet corn, asparagus, beans, potatoes, tomatoes, gherkins, herbs, harissa, sriracha, and mustard.
TRANSFORM	Turn mayo into aioli by combining crushed garlic, lemon juice, and salt, then adding mayo and Dijon mustard.
HACK	Mayo is the key to a crisp grilled cheese sandwich, so slather the outsides with the stuff before grilling.

Chicken kale Caesar

3 slices sourdough bread
1–2 tbsp. extra virgin
olive oil
2 garlic cloves, chopped
3 cups chopped kale
1½ tbsp. mayonnaise
1 tsp. capers, drained,
rinsed, and chopped
1 tsp. white wine vinegar
Half a lemon, juiced
1 cup cooked chicken
¼ cup Parmesan, shaved
Handful chopped chives

**Massaging the kale with oil and salt softens the leaves,
so don't skip this step.**

Preheat the oven to 400°F. Tear the bread into a baking dish, coat
in 1 tablespoon olive oil, sprinkle over some salt and the garlic, and
combine. Bake in a single layer for 15 minutes, turning occasionally,
until golden. Set aside to cool.

Put the kale in a large bowl, add a drizzle of oil and a pinch
of salt, and massage for a few minutes with your fingers. In a small
bowl, combine the mayonnaise, capers, vinegar, and lemon juice,
then tip over the kale and toss. Tear over the chicken, add the
croutons, and top with the Parmesan and chives. Serves 2-3.

Crab cocktail

1 large lettuce, shredded
Half a cucumber, peeled
into ribbons
3 large radishes, sliced
1 scallion, finely sliced
Small handful dill, chopped
Small handful parsley,
chopped
Drizzle of olive oil
Half a lemon, zested
and juiced
1½ tbsp. mayonnaise
2 tbsp. tomato ketchup
½ tsp. Worcestershire sauce
1½ cups white crab meat

**Swap shrimp for crab in this retro classic. The Marie Rose
sauce, however, is nonnegotiable.**

Put the first six ingredients in a serving bowl, drizzle with a little oil,
a squeeze of lemon, and season. Combine. In a small bowl, combine
the mayonnaise, ketchup, and Worcestershire sauce with a squeeze
of lemon juice and the zest. Mix in the crab meat, then tip over the
salad, and combine. Serves 2.

Celeriac and apple remoulade

2 apples, halved, cored, and sliced into sticks
1 lemon, juiced
Half a celeriac, peeled and grated
3 tbsp. mayonnaise
Handful chives, chopped or snipped with scissors
1 tbsp. wholegrain mustard
1 tbsp. cider vinegar

Tart from the apples, earthy from the celeriac: spoon this crunchy salad on the side of a roast chicken.

Put the apples in a bowl, squeeze over the lemon juice, then add the celeriac. In a small bowl, mix the remaining ingredients, then tip into the celeriac bowl, and combine. Season. Serves 4-6.

Aji verde

2–3 jalapeno chiles from a jar
1 large handful cilantro, leaves and stalks
Small handful mint
3 tbsp. mayonnaise
1 tbsp. lime juice
1 garlic clove, crushed

A take on the iconic Peruvian green sauce, ideal for a barbecue.

Put all the ingredients in a food processor with some salt and pepper, and a teaspoon of cold water. Blitz.

Broccoli Reuben pan bake

3½ cups broccoli florets, large ones chopped up
⅔ cup sauerkraut
1 small red onion, sliced
2 garlic cloves, crushed
2–3 tbsp. olive oil
3 slices rye bread
2½ tbsp. mayonnaise
1 tsp. sriracha
2 tsp. ketchup
2 gherkins, chopped

Court Street Grocers in New York makes an epic broccoli Reuben sandwich, which I've reimagined as a pan bake.

Preheat the oven to 400°F. Put the broccoli, sauerkraut, onion, garlic, 2 tablespoons olive oil, and some seasoning in a baking dish. Toss to coat, then roast for 20 minutes, stirring halfway through cooking. Meanwhile, tear the bread into a bowl and toss with a little oil and salt, then set aside. After the broccoli has had 20 minutes, tip over the croutons, and return to the oven for 10-15 minutes, until crisp and golden. Meanwhile, in a bowl, combine the remaining ingredients with some salt and pepper. To serve, drizzle the dressing over the pan bake. Serves 4.

Canned tuna

If you have a can of tuna, you have dinner. Its firm texture makes it ideal for those who don't like "fishy" fish, while its versatility knows no bounds: stuffed inside a sandwich, mashed into fishcakes, or flaked into pasta dishes and salads, while it keeps a degree of firmness when baked. This meaty fish, packed in brine, spring water, or oil, comes in steaks or flakes, and the price can vary greatly. For me, this is the place to spend a bit more, if you can, but eat a bit less, and always go for pole and line caught—it's better for the environment.

PAIR WITH	Anchovy, eggs, cheese, potatoes, spinach, asparagus, sweet potato, sweet corn, red pepper, tomatoes, arugula, chile, lemon, dill, parsley, olives, capers, white beans, and chickpeas.
TRANSFORM	Perfect for blending into dips with cannellini beans and lemon juice, or butter and capers. Spread on crispbread or serve with crudites.
HEALTH	Tuna is a good source of protein, low in fat, as well as containing vitamin B12.

Green goddess tuna sandwich

1 garlic clove, chopped
⅓ cup yogurt
2⅓ tbsp. mayonnaise
Large handful basil
Large handful parsley
Small handful tarragon
1 lemon, zest of half then juiced
1 tbsp. olive oil
1 can (7 oz.) tuna, drained
4 slices bread

Green goddess is a Californian classic, but it's good for so much more than dipping crudités—like in place of mayo in a tuna sandwich. You could also add some arugula or watercress if you fancy.

Put all the ingredients apart from the tuna and bread in a food processor and blitz. Season to taste. Break up the tuna with a fork, then add to the dressing. Pile onto two slices of bread and top with the other slices. Makes 2.

Tuna, crispy chickpea, and radicchio salad

14 oz. chickpeas (ideally from a jar)
2 tbsp. olive oil
1 garlic clove, minced
2 tbsp. red wine vinegar
1 tsp. golden honey
½ tsp. Dijon mustard
1 head radicchio, sliced
1 can (7 oz.) tuna, drained

Crispy chickpeas are great for adding texture to salads and soups, or simply to snack on, so it's a wise move to make more than you need.

Preheat the oven to 350°F. Drain the chickpeas, pat dry, and tip onto a baking sheet. Drizzle with 1 tablespoon olive oil, add the garlic, some seasoning, and toss. Roast for 15 minutes, stirring halfway through cooking, until crisp. Meanwhile, in a large bowl whisk the vinegar, honey, mustard, 1 tablespoon olive oil, and seasoning. Add the radicchio, chickpeas, and flake in the tuna, and toss. Serves 2.

Tuna tortilla

3 tbsp. olive oil
1 large white onion, finely sliced
1 garlic clove, minced
1 can (7 oz.) tuna, drained
Small handful parsley, chopped
6 eggs

Tortillas, or Spanish omelets, are quick, easy, and ideal for when you're running low on fresh ingredients. This tuna version is the perfect match for a tomato salad.

Heat 2 tablespoons olive oil in a large skillet, then add the onions and cook until soft—about 8 minutes. Add the garlic, cook for 2 minutes, then tip the lot into a bowl. Add the flaked tuna, parsley, and some seasoning. Beat the eggs, then tip into the tuna bowl. Heat 1 tablespoon olive oil in a skillet over high heat then add the egg mix, swirling around so it reaches the edges. Cook until just set, about 5 minutes, then cover the pan with a plate, flip out the tortilla, then slide it back into the pan. Cook for a few more minutes until done. Serves 2-4, depending on accompaniments.

Tuna stuffed peppers

2 red bell peppers, halved
  and seeded
1–2 tbsp. olive oil
9 oz. potatoes, chopped
1 can (7 oz.) tuna, drained
1 lemon, zested, juice
  of half
Dash of red wine vinegar
1 garlic clove, chopped
2 tbsp. pitted olives, chopped
Small handful basil,
  leaves torn

**Tuna and potatoes are a simple yet comforting
combo and make a hearty filling for red bell peppers.
Serve warm or at room temperature.**

Preheat the oven to 400°F. Put the peppers cut-side up in a
roasting pan, drizzle with a little oil, season, and bake for 20
minutes. Meanwhile, boil the potatoes in salted water until soft,
then mash. In a bowl, mash the drained tuna with 1 tablespoon
olive oil, the lemon zest and juice, and a dash of vinegar. Add the
potatoes, garlic, olives, torn basil leaves, and some seasoning, and
combine. Divide the mix between the pepper halves and return to
the oven for 10 minutes. Serves 2.

Tuna, tomato, and olive spaghetti

2 tbsp. olive oil
1 celery stalk, finely chopped
2 garlic cloves, finely chopped
Pinch of red pepper flakes
1 can (14½ oz.) chopped
  tomatoes
7 oz. spaghetti
1 can (7 oz.) tuna, drained
Handful pitted black olives,
  chopped
Small handful fresh oregano,
  chopped

**Let your pantry do the heavy lifting and make a double batch
of the sauce (before adding the tuna) to stick in the freezer
for the future.**

Heat the olive oil in a large saucepan, then add the celery, garlic,
chile, and tomatoes. Bring to a simmer, then cook for 10 minutes.
Meanwhile, cook the pasta according to the package instructions,
reserving some of the cooking water. Add the tuna, olives, and
seasoning. Transfer the pasta to the sauce with a splash of the
cooking water, and toss. Scatter over the oregano. Serves 2.

Black beans

Rich, creamy, earthy, yet slightly nutty, black beans are so versatile. While they're a staple of Central and South America, as well as being popular in creole and Caribbean fare, black beans should not be pigeonholed—they also welcome ingredients like citrus, tahini, and soy. The thing to remember about these beans, though, is that they take on the flavor of whatever they're cooked with, so don't hold back. You'll also want to hunt out fermented black beans, which are often used in Huanese dishes. Rich in umami, they pack a punch; eat with chicken, pork, or seafood, with lots of garlic, ginger, and chile.

PAIR WITH	Chicken, beef, pork, avocado, eggs, feta, tomatoes, sweet potato, kale, sweet corn, celeriac, pineapple, chile, lime, cilantro, cumin, quinoa, tahini, and soy sauce.
TRANSFORM	For easy refried beans, cook onion in a little oil until soft, then add garlic, chile, and cumin, followed by drained black beans, a little of the can liquid, paprika, and salt. Mash and serve with chopped cilantro, alongside tostadas.
HEALTH	A good source of fiber, protein, and folate.

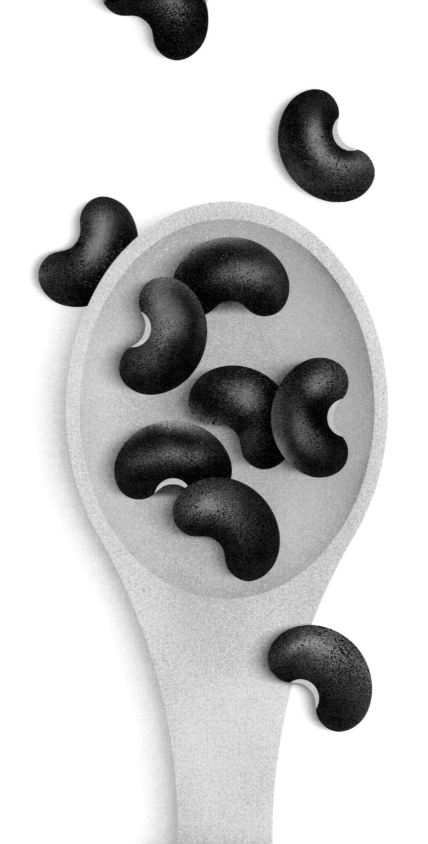

Broccoli and black bean noodles

3 tsp. tahini
3 tsp. soy sauce
2 tsp. golden honey
3 tsp. rice vinegar
1 tsp. chili oil
½ tsp. sesame oil
1 garlic clove, minced
1 lime, juiced
1 head broccoli, separated
   into florets
2 nests egg noodles
2 cups black beans, drained
   and rinsed
1 scallion, finely sliced

Black beans are a good foil for punchy Asian sauces with lots of chile and lime.

In a large bowl, combine the tahini, soy sauce, honey, rice vinegar, chili oil, sesame oil, and minced garlic with a good squeeze of lime juice. Taste and adjust with more lime juice, if needed. In a saucepan of boiling salted water, cook the broccoli florets for 3 minutes. Add the noodles and cook for another 5 minutes (or according to the package instructions), adding the drained beans in the last minutes. Drain and toss in the dressing, then eat topped with the scallions. Serves 2.

Huevos rancheros-style scramble

1 onion, sliced
1 large garlic clove, sliced
1 red chile, chopped
1 red pepper, sliced
2 bay leaves
1 tsp. paprika
Drizzle of oil
1 can (14½ oz.) chopped
   tomatoes
2 cups black beans, drained
   and rinsed
Big handful spinach
4 eggs, lightly beaten
Corn tortillas, to serve
Handful cilantro leaves,
   to serve
Shredded Cheddar, to serve

If you've got any jarred red bell peppers that need using, chuck them in instead of fresh. This is also a good moment to use up a half-can of black beans.

Fry the onion, garlic, chile, peppers, bay leaves, and paprika in a little oil for 5 minutes. Add the tomatoes, beans, ½ cup water, and some seasoning, and simmer for 10 minutes. Stir through the spinach to wilt, then tip in the eggs, and scramble over a low heat. Spoon onto warmed corn tortillas and scatter over the cilantro and Cheddar. Serves 2.

Black bean, tahini and chile dip

1 can (15 oz.) black beans,
  drained and rinsed
1 garlic clove
1 lime, zest of half
  then juiced
3 tbsp. tahini
Half a green chile
Handful cilantro leaves

When faced with surplus ingredients, dips are always a good idea, and tahini and lime perk up black beans perfectly.

Put the black beans in a food processor with 3 tablespoons water, and blitz smooth. Add the garlic, lime juice and zest, tahini, chile, cilantro, and a pinch of salt, and blitz again. Serves 4.

Sweet corn and black bean taco salad

Half a red chile, chopped
2 limes, juiced, plus zest of 1
2 tsp. olive oil
Handful cilantro leaves,
  chopped
1 romaine lettuce, sliced
3 scallions, sliced
1 cup sweet corn, drained
2 cups black beans, drained
  and rinsed
10 cherry tomatoes,
  quartered
1 avocado, diced
3 taco shells

All the flavors of a taco in salad form.

In a large bowl, combine the chile, lime juice and zest, oil, cilantro, and a pinch of salt. Add the lettuce, scallions, sweet corn, black beans, cherry tomatoes, and avocado, toss, and set aside. Heat the taco shells in the oven, then leave to cool a little before crumbling into the salad. Toss again and serve. Serves 4.

Black bean and sweet potato pie

2 lb. 3 oz. sweet potatoes,
  chopped into chunks
1 red onion, chopped
2 garlic cloves, chopped
Olive oil
1 tsp. ground cumin
1 tsp. ground cilantro
2 tsp. smoked paprika
2⅔ cups cremini mushrooms,
  cut into chunks
1 can (15 oz.) black beans,
  drained and rinsed
1 can (14 oz.) puy lentils,
  drained
1 tsp. bouillon powder
1 can (14½ oz.) chopped
  tomatoes
1 tbsp. tomato paste
Soy sauce
⅔ cup feta

This freezes well, so it's worth making a double batch—hold back the feta until just before you bake it, though.

Cook the sweet potato in salted boiling water until tender, about 15 minutes. Drain then mash with some seasoning. Meanwhile, fry the onion and garlic in a splash of oil for 5 minutes, then add the spices. Stir in the mushrooms, beans, lentils, and the broth. Continue cooking for 10 minutes, then add the canned tomato, tomato paste, and a splash of soy, and simmer for 10 minutes. Preheat the oven to 400°F. Tip the mixture into a baking dish and top with the mashed potato. Crumble over the feta and bake for 30 minutes. Serves 4–6.

Mustard

Whether you play it bold or stick to the smallest hit, mustard really brings swagger to a dish, both hot and cold. I don't think anyone has ever regretted adding a teaspoon or two of Dijon or wholegrain mustard to soups, gratins, or glazes for meats. I rarely make a vinaigrette that doesn't involve a couple of teaspoons of the stuff. Made by combining the ground seeds of the mustard plant (of which there are black, brown, white, and yellow) with the likes of water, vinegar, and flour, there are some dishes that are just inconceivable without a kick of mustard.

VARIETIES	First made in Dijon, France, the mustard of the same name is robust, sharp, and pungent, making it ideal for vinaigrettes and sauces. Whole grain is made with unground mustard seeds so has a coarser texture; bright yellow mustard has the addition of turmeric, is mellow in flavor, and essential when it comes to hot dogs; dry mustard powder will invariably improve a cheese sauce.
PAIRS WITH	Celeriac, cabbage, leeks, beet, potato, mushroom, carrot, sprouts, chicken, ham, sausages, pork chops, cold meats, apple, salmon, lentils, honey, cider, and cheese.
TRANSFORM	Dijon is used to make a classic vinaigrette: whisk 2 teaspoons mustard, 2 tablespoons red or white wine vinegar and a pinch of sugar. Season, then gradually add 6 tablespoons extra virgin olive oil. Then take it in any direction you fancy: add lemon juice, shallots, anchovies, or capers, or switch up the vinegar (sherry vinegar is a good bet).

Herby leeks and eggs

2 eggs
2 large leeks, cut into rings
1 tbsp. olive oil
1½ tbsp. mayonnaise
1 tsp. Dijon mustard
1 tsp. chopped tarragon
1 tsp. chopped chives
1 tsp. chopped flat-leaf
  parsley
3 cornichons, diced
2 slices of toast

**This lurks in the egg mayonnaise and gribiche family.
The egg cooking time is for jammy yolks, so adjust according
to your preference.**

Boil the eggs in simmering water for 7 minutes, then drain and run
under cold water. Once cool, peel. Fry the leeks in the olive oil until
completely soft. Turn off the heat, add the mayonnaise, mustard,
chopped herbs, and cornichons. Season to taste, then divide the leek
mixture between the toasts. Cut the eggs in half, place on top of each
toast, and add a grind or two of black pepper. Serves 2.

Balsamic and mustard pork chops

1 tbsp. olive oil
1 tbsp. balsamic vinegar
1 tsp. wholegrain mustard
1 garlic clove, crushed
Small handful chopped
  rosemary
1 pork chop

**An easy dinner to serve alongside vegetables. Just be
sure to leave enough time to marinate the meat.**

Preheat the oven to 400°F. In a small bowl, combine the olive oil,
balsamic vinegar, mustard, garlic, and rosemary. Season the pork
chop, then transfer to a baking dish. Tip over the marinade, turning
the chop over to coat it, then cover and put in the refrigerator for
1 hour. Bake for 20 minutes, or until cooked through. Serves 1.

Tahini-mustard dressing

3 tbsp. tahini
1 tbsp. Dijon mustard
1 tbsp. maple syrup
1 tbsp. soy sauce

**A good thing to have up your sleeve, as it works as a salad
dressing and on roast veg, such as butternut squash or cabbage.**

In a small bowl, combine all the ingredients with 1 tablespoon water.
Taste and adjust as needed.

Beet burgers

2⅓ cups grated beets
Drizzle of oil
3 scallions, finely chopped
1 garlic clove, crushed
Handful mint, chopped
Handful dill, chopped
1 lemon, zested, and
  the juice from half
1 tbsp. wholegrain mustard
2¼ cups fresh bread
  crumbs
1⅓ cups feta
Spoonful hummus, to serve

These burgers freeze well, so it's worth making a double batch for future meals.

Preheat the oven to 400°F. Squeeze as much liquid from the beets as you can. Heat a little oil in a saucepan, then add the beets, scallions, and garlic, cooking until the beet breaks down—about 5 minutes. Tip into a bowl and add the mint and dill, lemon zest and juice, mustard, bread crumbs, and some seasoning. Crumble in the feta, combine, then shape into four patties. Transfer to a lined cookie sheet and cook for 25 minutes. Serve topped with a good spoonful of hummus. Makes 4.

Cauliflower toad

1¼ cups all-purpose flour
3 eggs
⅞ cup milk
2 tbsp. wholegrain mustard
1 large cauliflower, cut into
  florets
2 red onions, cut into sixths
1 tsp. dried sage
1 tsp. paprika
3 tbsp. olive oil
½ cup shredded Cheddar

Cauliflower takes the place of sausages in this comforting classic. Just add onion gravy.

Preheat the oven to 425°F. In a large bowl, whisk the flour, eggs, and some seasoning until smooth. Stir in the milk and 1 tablespoon mustard, then put in the refrigerator to rest for 1 hour. Put the cauliflower florets in a roasting pan with the onion, sage, paprika, and some salt and pepper. Add the olive oil, give everything a good mix, then roast for 25 minutes.

Meanwhile, combine the Cheddar with 1 tablespoon mustard in a small bowl. Remove the cauliflower from the oven, tip the rested batter over the top, and scatter with the cheese mix. Return to the oven for 20-25 minutes, until risen, golden, and crisp. Serves 4 as a main, 6 as a side.

Rice

When it comes to versatility, rice is tops. From basmati and jasmine, to arborio, calasparra (used in paella) and sushi, rice can transport you to wherever you want to go, spanning across breakfast (the Chinese porridge congee or fried with egg, for example), lunch, and dinner. It's just as happy accessorized with spices, shrimps, or kimchi as it is simply boiled and buttered—however, as is so often the case, simplicity can be the hardest thing to pull off. When cooking on the stovetop, one cup of basmati or white rice to two cups of water should see you right, but be sure to rinse it beforehand to get rid of any excess starch. Short-grain rice (think risotto, paella), however, needs that starch to achieve the desired creaminess, so rinsing is not needed.

VARIETIES	Fine, long-grain rice, like basmati, is mainly used in Indian and Iranian dishes, such as biryanis, while short, plump grains like arborio, sushi rice, and calasparra bring creaminess or stickiness to, say, risotto or sushi. That said, Thai jasmine rice is slightly sticky but would be considered long grain.
TRANSFORM	The texture of basmati rice will be greatly improved by letting it stand, covered, for 10 minutes after cooking.
HACK	If you want to make large quantities of basmati rice, try baking it in the oven—you'll get a better result.

Gingery carrot and rice soup

2 tbsp. olive oil
1 onion, sliced
4½ cup carrots, grated
1 thumb-size piece ginger, minced
2 garlic cloves, finely chopped
2 tsp. turmeric
½ cup basmati rice
4 cups broth

Essentially a soup in which you cook rice, it's a nourishing bowl for a cold day.

Heat the oil in a large saucepan, then add the onion and carrots and cook, stirring occasionally, for 10 minutes. Stir in the ginger, garlic and turmeric, and cook for another few minutes. Add the rice, stirring to coat, then add the broth. Cover and cook for 10 minutes, then season with black pepper. Serves 4.

Herb and pistachio pilaf

2 tbsp. mixed herbs (mint, basil, dill)
Half a green chile
1 tsp. white miso
2 limes, juiced (about 4 tsp.)
3 tbsp. olive oil
1½ cups sugar snap peas, sliced diagonally
4 scallions, chopped
⅓ cup pistachios, toasted and chopped
2 garlic cloves, crushed
½ cup basmati rice
2 cups broth

Turn this vibrant green pilaf into more of a meal by stirring through shredded cooked chicken.

Blend the herbs, chile, miso, lime juice, and some seasoning in a food processor, then drizzle in 2 tablespoons oil and blend again. In a bowl, combine the sugar snap peas, scallions, and pistachios. Heat 1 tablespoon olive oil in a saucepan, then add the garlic and rice, stir for a minute, then pour in the broth, and season with black pepper. Bring to a boil, cover, and cook for 15 minutes, or until the liquid has almost been absorbed. Turn off the heat, stir through the herb mix, then cover and leave for 10 minutes. Stir through the sugar snap pea mix. Serves 2.

Baked leek and bacon rice

Drizzle of olive oil
½ cup bacon, diced
2 leeks, finely sliced
2 garlic cloves, finely chopped
1 tsp. paprika
2 sprigs thyme, leaves chopped
¾ cup paella rice
1 can (14½ oz.) chopped tomatoes
2 cups broth
Small handful parsley, chopped
Wedge of lemon, to serve

A low-maintenance, no-fuss dinner that's good on its own, or with a bitter leaf salad or poached egg.

Preheat the oven to 400°F. Add a little oil to an ovenproof pan, add the bacon and cook until golden. Add the leeks and garlic, cook until soft then stir in the paprika, thyme, rice, chopped tomatoes, broth, and some black pepper. Bring to a boil, then turn off the heat, and bake, covered, for 25 minutes, until the rice is cooked, and the liquid has almost all been absorbed. Leave to rest for 5 minutes, before serving with the parsley scattered over and a lemon wedge on the side. Serves 2, generously.

Sushi salad bowl

1 cup sushi rice
2 tbsp. soy sauce
2 tbsp. rice vinegar
1 tsp. golden honey
1 tbsp. sesame oil
½ tsp. wasabi paste
1 lemon
2¼ cups broccolini, cooked
½ cup frozen edamame
  beans, cooked
1 avocado, thinly sliced
1 carrot, peeled into ribbons
Pickled ginger, to serve
1 nori sheet, snipped with
  scissors
1 scallion, thinly sliced
Sesame seeds, toasted,
  to serve

You can customize this to make it your own, adding whatever veg, pickles, meat, or fish you like.

Rinse the rice then cook according to the package instructions. Meanwhile, in a bowl combine the soy sauce, vinegar, honey, sesame oil, wasabi paste, and a squeeze of lemon. Once the rice is cooked, stir through a couple of tablespoons of dressing, and split between two bowls. Arrange the broccolini, edamame, avocado, carrot, and pickled ginger around the rice, spoon over some more dressing, and top with the nori, scallion, and toasted sesame seeds. Serves 2.

Squash, sage, and chestnut rice

1 medium butternut
  squash, peeled, and cut
  into chunks
Small handful sage,
  chopped
2 tbsp. olive oil
1 litre broth
1 onion, finely chopped
2 garlic cloves, finely
  chopped
1½ cups arborio rice
⅝ cup white wine
1 cup cooked chestnuts,
  quartered
½ cup Parmesan, grated

Go the whole hog and crown your rice with a handful of crispy sage leaves.

Heat the oven to 400°F. Put the squash on a roasting pan with the sage and some seasoning. Add 1 tablespoon oil, toss, and roast for 45 minutes until soft and caramelized.

Bring the broth to a boil in a saucepan, then lower the heat and simmer. Add 1 tablespoon oil to a large saucepan and cook the onion until soft, about 8 minutes. Add the garlic, cook for 2 minutes, then stir in the rice and cook for a few minutes. Pour in the wine and let it bubble away until evaporated, then add the broth a ladleful at a time, waiting for the liquid to be absorbed before adding more. Keep going until the rice is cooked, adding the chestnuts with the last ladleful of liquid. Mash the roast squash, then stir through the rice, followed by the Parmesan. Season with black pepper. Serves 4.

Pearl barley

Barley has something of an image problem, but it's a real workhorse, especially when it's cold outside. Nutritious with a nutty flavor and chewy texture, pearl barley adds bulk and a beautiful creaminess to soups, stews, and salads. It comes in two forms: hulled (pot), and pearl (or pearled). The difference is that hulled has had the hull removed but the bran around the grain remains (meaning more nutrients, but a longer cooking time); pearl barley, which is more commonly used, has had the bran removed, giving it a pale color and a less chewy texture but it cooks faster, which you do by simmering in broth or water. As it swells during cooking, it makes a good alternative to rice in dishes like risotto or even rice pudding, but remember it's a sponge, meaning it's at its best when it can absorb lots of flavor.

PAIR WITH	Beef, chicken, chorizo, bacon, feta, butternut squash, beet, kale, mushrooms, zucchini, Swiss chard, peas, sweet corn, leek, parsnip, fava beans, carrots, tomatoes, lemon, preserved lemon, cranberry, orange, apples, peaches, and chickpeas.
TRANSFORM	Adding cooked pearl barley to burgers, whether meat or vegetarian, adds great texture while keeping things tender.
HACK	Add a couple of tbsp. of pearl barley to a hot, dry skillet and toast for a few minutes, until fragrant. Once cool, crush in a mortar and use to top salads.

PEARL BARLEY

ORGANIC

Parsnip, apple and barley soup

3½ cups parsnips, chopped
3 tbsp. olive oil
4 cups broth
½ cup pearl barley
1 onion, finely chopped
1 large garlic clove, minced
1 apple, cored and chopped
2 sprigs thyme, leaves only

When reheating any leftovers, be sure to add a splash of water to loosen.

Preheat the oven to 425°F. Put the parsnips on a baking sheet, toss with 2 tablespoons oil and some seasoning, then roast for 30 minutes. Put the broth in a saucepan and bring to a simmer. Add the pearl barley and simmer for 30 minutes, then strain, catching the broth in a pitcher underneath. Top the broth up with boiling water so you have 3¼ cups. Meanwhile, heat 1 tablespoon oil in a saucepan and cook the onion with a pinch of salt until softened. Stir in the garlic, cook for a minute, then add the apple, roast parsnip, and thyme. Pour over the broth, simmer for 10 minutes, then blend. Stir in the barley, and season with black pepper. Serves 4.

Pearl barley, smoked mackerel, and beet salad

2 cups broth
½ cup pearl barley
⅔ cup yogurt
Half a lemon, zest and juice
1 tbsp. olive oil
1 tsp. nigella seeds
Small handful cilantro, chopped
Small handful mint, chopped
1 apple, cut into sticks
1½ cups arugula
1 medium-size cooked beet, diced
2 smoked mackerel fillets, broken into chunks
2 tsp. toasted sunflower seeds

It's worth keeping an eye on the liquid levels when cooking the barley, topping up with a little more broth if needed.

Put the broth in a saucepan and bring to a boil. Add the pearl barley, then lower the heat, and simmer for 20 minutes, until the broth has been absorbed and the barley is cooked. Leave to cool a little. Meanwhile, in a small bowl, combine the yogurt, lemon zest and a good squeeze of juice, olive oil, nigella seeds, and herbs. Put the apple in a serving dish, squeeze over a little lemon, then add the barley, arugula, beet, and mackerel. Toss, top with the sunflower seeds, and serve with the yogurt. Serves 2.

Chorizo pearl barley with a fried egg

½ cup chorizo, sliced
1 onion, finely chopped
1 garlic clove, minced
¾ cup pearl barley
1 tbsp. tomato paste
⅓ cup white wine
2½ cups broth
½ cup frozen peas
Large handful parsley, chopped
2 eggs

Everything is better topped with an egg. Any leftover barley will make for a superior lunchbox the next day.

Fry the chorizo in a skillet until golden, then transfer to a plate, and set aside. Add the onion, cook for 5 minutes, then stir through the garlic, and continue cooking for a minute. Add the pearl barley and tomato paste, stir to coat, then tip in the wine and let it bubble until it has evaporated. Add the broth and a good grind of black pepper, and simmer until the liquid has been absorbed—about 30 minutes. Stir in the chorizo, peas, and parsley, and heat through while you fry the eggs in a large skillet. Divide the pearl barley between two bowls and top each with an egg. Serves 2.

Pearl barley pudding with pears and honey

⅔ cup pearl barley
3 cups milk of your choice
½ tsp. vanilla bean paste
1 cinnamon stick
1½ tbsp. superfine sugar
1 pear, sliced
Handful pistachios, chopped
Golden honey, to serve

This sits in the same realm as rice pudding, but a topping of sliced pear, pistachios, and golden honey makes it breakfast appropriate.

Rinse the pearl barley, then put in a medium saucepan with the milk, vanilla, cinnamon, sugar, and a pinch of salt. Bring to a boil then turn down the heat and simmer, stirring occasionally, for 30 minutes, until the barley is cooked. Spoon into bowls and top with the sliced pear, pistachios, and a good drizzle of honey. Serves 2.

Pearl barley with feta and roast mushrooms

2¾ cups portabello mushrooms, torn into chunks
2 sprigs thyme, leaves only
1 garlic clove, crushed
1½ tbsp. olive oil
1 onion, chopped
1¾ cups broth
⅔ cup pearl barley
¼ cup feta
½ preserved lemon, skin finely chopped
Handful parsley, chopped

The sharp saltiness of feta is a fine match for meaty roast mushrooms.

Preheat the oven to 400°F. Put the mushrooms in a baking dish with the thyme leaves and garlic. Drizzle with oil, season, and toss. Roast until tender, about 25 minutes. Meanwhile, heat the olive oil in a large saucepan, then add the onion and cook until soft. Pour in the broth, bring to a boil, then add the barley and simmer until tender and the liquid has been mostly (but not completely) absorbed. Stir through the feta, preserved lemon, and parsley, and season. Serve topped with the roast mushrooms. Serves 2.

Couscous

Although treated like a grain, couscous is in fact dried and cracked pasta made from semolina. A staple in North Africa, most of the couscous you'll find in shops is ready-cooked and dried, meaning it simply requires soaking in liquid to transform into something light and fluffy. Its short cooking time (about five minutes) means it's a near-instant accompaniment to braises, stews, and roast vegetables, while its nutty, sweet flavor earns it a place as the base in colorful salads with tomatoes, roast zucchini, or eggplants—topping with slices of fried halloumi is optional but very much encouraged.

VARIETIES	Moroccan, which is the smallest and just a fraction larger than semolina; Israeli or pearl couscous, which is larger; and Lebanese, being the largest and therefore taking the longest to cook. You'll also find whole-wheat couscous, which is made from whole-wheat durum flour.
TRANSFORM	If you don't have broth to hand, infuse water with crushed garlic, ginger, and maybe an onion.
HACK	Make sure you take a moment to properly fluff the couscous to avoid clumps, which is best done with your hands (be sure the couscous has cooled).

Brothy harissa couscous and chicken

A good place to use up any leftover chicken from a weekend roast.

1 tbsp. olive oil
1 onion, chopped
1 garlic clove, sliced
1 fennel bulb, chopped
2½ cups broth
1 tbsp. harissa
½ cup giant couscous
¾ cup snow peas, sliced on the diagonal
2 handfuls spinach
½ cup cooked chicken, shredded

In a heavy-bottomed saucepan, heat the olive oil and cook the onion, garlic, and fennel until soft—about 10 minutes. Add the broth and harissa and bring to a boil. Tip in the couscous and simmer, covered, for 5 minutes. Stir in the snow peas, cook for 2 minutes, then stir through the spinach and chicken, and cook for another 5 minutes. Ladle into bowls. Serves 2.

Pea, bean, and broccoli couscous with pistou

The real star here is the pistou, which is a relative of basil pesto (minus the pine nuts).

1 small garlic clove
½ cup basil
1 tbsp. olive oil
2 tbsp. Parmesan, grated
2 cups broth
2¼ cups broccolini, chopped
½ cup frozen fava beans
¾ cup frozen peas
1 lemon
½ cup couscous

In a pestle and mortar, pound the garlic, basil, olive oil, and a pinch of salt, followed by the Parmesan. Heat the broth in a large saucepan, then add the broccolini and cook for 3 minutes. Add the fava beans and peas, cook for 2-3 minutes until tender, then stir through the pistou, a squeeze of lemon, and some seasoning. Stir through the couscous, cover, and remove from the heat. Leave to stand for 5 minutes. Serves 2.

Packed lunch couscous in a jar

There's an order to layering a jarred salad as you don't want it to end up soggy. Remember: wet things at the bottom, crunchy things at the top.

⅓ cup couscous
½ cup broth
Small handful dill, chopped
Small handful mint, chopped
Small handful walnuts, chopped
3 dried apricots, chopped
1 beet, grated
1 handful spinach
½ cup goat cheese, crumbled
1 tbsp. olive oil
Half a lemon, juiced
1 tsp. golden honey

Put the couscous in a bowl, pour over the broth, cover, and set aside for 5 minutes. Stir through the herbs, walnuts, and apricots, and season with black pepper. Divide the couscous between two jars. Top with the beet, followed by the spinach and cheese. In a small jar, combine the oil, lemon juice, honey, and seasoning. To serve, pour over the dressing and toss. Serves 2.

Spanakopita zucchini boats

⅓ cup couscous
½ cup broth
2 zucchini, halved, and middle scooped out
1–2 tbsp. olive oil
1 garlic clove, chopped
4 scallions, chopped
2 handfuls spinach
½ cup feta, crumbled
1 lemon, zested
Handful dill, chopped
Handful mint, chopped

The flavors of this classic Greek pie are housed in hollowed-out zucchini halves, which makes a pleasing lunch when served with a tomato salad.

Preheat the oven to 425°F. Put the couscous in a heatproof bowl, pour over the broth, cover, and leave to stand for 5 minutes. Fluff up. Meanwhile, chop the scooped-out zucchini flesh. Add 1 tablespoon olive oil to a skillet, then add the garlic, scallion, chopped zucchini, and some seasoning, and cook for 5 minutes. Stir in the spinach to wilt, then add the cooked couscous, feta, lemon zest, and herbs. Put the zucchini halves on a baking sheet, then spoon in the couscous filling. Drizzle with oil, then bake for 25–30 minutes, until the zucchini are cooked through. Serves 2–3.

Couscous kedgeree with chickpeas

1 tbsp. olive oil
1 onion, chopped
1 garlic clove, chopped
1 thumb-size piece of ginger, chopped
1 bay leaf
2 tsp. curry powder
3 red bell peppers from a jar, chopped
½ cup frozen peas
2½ cups broth
1 cup couscous
1 jar (11½ oz.) chickpeas, drained and rinsed
Half a lemon, juiced
Handful cilantro, chopped
2 eggs, boiled for 7 minutes, plunged into cold water, peeled then halved

Traditionally made with rice, couscous adds a nice textural change. Bulk it up even more by topping with flaked kippers.

Heat the olive oil in a skillet, add the onion, garlic, ginger, and bay leaf, and cook until the onion is soft. Add the curry powder, cook for 1 minute, then add the peppers, peas, broth, and couscous. Bring to a boil, cover, and cook until the liquid has been absorbed—about 6 minutes. Season, stir through the chickpeas to heat, then add the lemon juice and cilantro. Top with the halved eggs. Serves 2.

Chickpea flour

Also known as garbanzo, gram (or Bengal gram) flour, and besan flour, chickpea flour is made by blitzing dried chickpeas into a fine powder. While the talents of this gluten-free, nutty, earthy flour are many, and can take you from Italy to India and the Middle East, it's worth noting that it won't rise in the same way as other flours or give you a light crumb. Chickpea flour does, however, really shine in pancakes, aka your fast-track weeknight dinner that simply requires flour, olive oil, water, and salt—although you can customize it with ingredients like ground turmeric or cumin.

TRANSFORM	A good option for making vegan, gluten-free Yorkshire puddings when combined with aquafaba (chickpea water).
HEALTH	Gluten-free, rich in fiber and minerals, such as potassium, and higher in protein than wheat flour.
HACK	Chickpea flour is a good binder and thickener, making it a good option for fritters and soups.

Aloo tikki

1 lb. Yukon Gold potatoes, cut into chunks
1–2 tbsp. oil
1 red onion, finely chopped
1 thumb-size piece of ginger, grated
1 green chile, chopped
1 tsp. garam masala
1 tsp. cinnamon
2 tbsp. chickpea (garbanzo) flour
Handful mint, chopped
Handful cilantro, chopped

These are ideal for lunch boxes and welcome a good spoonful of chutney.

Cook the potatoes in boiling water until tender, then drain and leave to steam dry. Meanwhile, heat a little oil in a saucepan, then fry the onion, ginger, and chile until soft, about 8 minutes. Stir in the spices, then remove from the heat. Mash the potato, then stir in the onion mix, flour, herbs, and some seasoning. Form into six to eight patties. Heat 1 tablespoon oil in a skillet and cook for 4 minutes on each side until golden. Makes 6-8.

Olive and sun-dried tomato farinata

2¾ cups chickpea (garbanzo) flour
2 cups water
2–3 tbsp. olive oil
2 red onions, finely sliced
Red pepper flakes
1 tbsp. chopped rosemary leaves
1 tsp. baking powder
¾ cup sun-dried tomatoes packed in oil, drained and sliced
⅔ cup pitted black olives, halved

Top this like you would pizza, then slice and serve alongside soups.

In a large bowl, mix the flour with a big pinch of salt. Make a well in the middle, pour in the water, and whisk until you have a batter. Cover and set aside for 2 hours. Put a little oil in a saucepan, then fry the onions with a pinch of red pepper flakes, the rosemary, and some seasoning until the onions are soft. Set aside to cool a little. Meanwhile, whisk 2 tablespoons olive oil and 1 teaspoon baking powder into the batter, followed by the onion mix. Preheat the oven to 475°F. Line a large baking sheet with parchment paper, brush with a little oil, then pour in the batter. Top with the tomatoes and black olives, then bake for 15-20 minutes, until golden. Serves 10-12.

Baked pea falafel

2⅓ cups frozen peas, cooked
9 oz. jarred chickpeas, drained
1 shallot, chopped
2 garlic cloves, chopped
2 tbsp. chickpea (garbanzo) flour
Small handful mint, chopped
Small handful parsley, chopped
Squeeze of lemon juice
½ tsp. baking powder
½ tsp. ground cumin
½ tsp. ground cilantro
Pinch of red pepper flakes
Oil, for baking

If the mixture is looking crumbly after blending, add a splash of water and blend again.

Preheat the oven to 425°F. Put all the ingredients apart from the oil in a food processor, season, and blend—you want it to still have some texture. Roll into balls, gently flatten, and transfer to a lined baking sheet. Drizzle with oil, then bake for 20 minutes, until crisp. Makes 8-10.

Chickpea pancakes with Swiss chard and salted ricotta

2¼ cups chickpea (garbanzo) flour
2–3 tbsp. olive oil
Small handful basil, chopped
Small handful parsley, chopped
1 onion, diced
1 garlic clove, crushed
2¾ cups Swiss chard, leaves shredded
1 lemon, zested
¼ cup salted ricotta, crumbled

These are so quick to make, and you can mix up the fillings depending on what's to hand (spinach or kale, say).

Whisk the flour with 1¼ cups water, 1 tablespoon olive oil, and most of the herbs. Season, and set aside. Meanwhile, heat 1 tablespoon oil in a saucepan, then add the onion and cook until soft. Add the garlic, cook for a minute, then add the Swiss chard and continue cooking until wilted. Stir through the lemon zest, some black pepper, and the remaining herbs. Heat a nonstick skillet over high heat, then add a little oil. Once hot, add half the batter and cook until set around the edges—a couple of minutes. Flip and cook on the other side for a few minutes. Repeat with the remaining batter. To serve, spoon the Swiss chard onto half of each pancake, top with the ricotta, then fold over. Serves 2.

Gluten-free bechamel

2 cups whole milk
1 bay leaf
Half an onion
3½ tbsp. butter
2½ tbsp. chickpea (garbanzo) flour
Grating of nutmeg

The milk really benefits from being left to infuse, ideally for half an hour.

In a saucepan, warm the milk, bay leaf, and onion until almost boiling. Remove from the heat and set aside. In a heavy-bottomed saucepan, melt the butter, then, once foaming, whisk in the flour until it smells biscuity. Remove the bay leaf and onion from the milk, then whisk a little of the milk into the flour. Pour in the rest of the milk, whisking continuously, until thickened. Add a grating of nutmeg and season. Serves 4-6.

Red split lentils

For me, red lentils mean dal and I'm guilty of stopping there. A member of the legume family, red lentils sustain and nourish, and tend to cook quite quickly (in about 15–20 minutes), making them a go-to for midweek dinners. Once cooked, they become thick and soothing, which is why they are so excellent in dals, curries (think cauliflower, spinach, sweet potato, chicken), and soups bolstered with spices. Red lentils (like all lentils) love company, absorbing any sharpness or spice they're exposed to, so think about what flavors you throw at them. And while they don't need soaking, you'll want to give them a good rinse before cooking to get rid of any dust.

PAIR WITH	Eggs, cauliflower, butternut squash, sweet potato, carrot, spinach, eggplant, broccoli, tomatoes, coconut, chile, ginger, chickpeas, cumin, cilantro, turmeric, and cardamom.
HEALTH	High in protein, iron, and fiber, they're also a source of B vitamins.
HACK	Red lentils don't like to be cooked in too much water, otherwise their nutrients leach out—you want just enough liquid that the lentils soak it up.

Baked lemon lentils and kale

1 tbsp. olive oil
1 onion, thinly sliced
1 garlic clove, chopped
1 thumb-size piece ginger, minced
1 tsp. ground cumin
1 tsp. turmeric
1 lemon, zested and juiced
¾ cup red split lentils
2½ cups broth
1 cup chopped kale

This is the ultimate bowl food, and the contrast of soft, lemony lentils with crisp, roasted kale is hard to beat.

Warm the olive oil in an ovenproof pan, then cook the onion until soft. Add the garlic and ginger, cook for 2 minutes, then stir in the cumin, turmeric, and some seasoning. Add the lemon juice and zest followed by the lentils and broth. Bring to a simmer, then cover, and bake at 400°C for 25 minutes. Meanwhile, tear the kale leaves into pieces, then rub in a little oil and a pinch of salt. Once the lentils have had their 25 minutes, tip the kale on top and return, uncovered, to the oven for 5 minutes. Serves 2–3.

Tomato and coconut lentils

1 tbsp. olive oil
1 large onion, chopped
2 garlic cloves, chopped
1 thumb-size piece ginger, grated
1 tbsp. curry powder
Red pepper flakes
¾ cup red split lentils
1 can (14½ oz.) chopped tomatoes
2 cups broth
1 cup coconut milk
Handful cilantro leaves, chopped
Half a lime, juiced
5 radishes, sliced, to serve

The sliced radish brings a welcome contrast to the creamy lentils.

Heat the oil in a large, heavy-bottomed saucepan, and cook the onions with a pinch of salt until soft. Stir in the garlic, ginger, curry powder, and a good pinch of red pepper flakes, and cook for 1 minute. Add the lentils, chopped tomatoes, broth, and a good grind of black pepper. Add the coconut milk, bring to a boil, then simmer for 25–30 minutes until the lentils are cooked. Check the seasoning, then stir through the cilantro and lime juice. Eat topped with the radishes. Serves 4.

Lentil-stuffed sweet potatoes

2 sweet potatoes, scrubbed
1 tbsp. olive oil
1 small red onion, diced
2 garlic cloves, crushed
1 thumb-size piece ginger, chopped
1 red chile, chopped
1 tsp. turmeric
1 tsp. cumin seeds
½ cup red split lentils
1½ cups broth
2 handfuls spinach
Cilantro leaves, to serve

Creamy on the inside, crisp on the outside, serve these roast sweet potatoes with yogurt, which you can dress up with scallion, chile, or herbs.

Preheat the oven to 400°F. Put the sweet potatoes on a baking sheet, drizzle with oil, and sprinkle with a large pinch of salt and pepper. Bake until tender, about 45 minutes. Meanwhile, in a saucepan, heat some oil and cook the onion with a pinch of salt until soft. Stir in the garlic, ginger, and chile, cook for 1 minute, then add the spices, and continue cooking for another minute. Pour in the lentils and broth, and simmer for 20-25 minutes. Stir through the spinach to wilt. To serve, put a sweet potato on two plates, split open, and pull apart a little. Spoon over the lentils and scatter with cilantro. Serves 2.

Zucchini and lentil fritters

½ cup red split lentils, rinsed
1 medium zucchini
1 red onion
1 red chile, roughly chopped
1 garlic clove, crushed
1 thumb-size piece ginger, roughly chopped
Large handful cilantro, chopped
Coconut oil

Soaking the lentils for at least an hour is essential, otherwise the cooked fritters will be hard.

In a bowl, soak the lentils in 1½ cups water for at least an hour. Grate the zucchini and onion into another bowl, sprinkle with salt, and set aside. Once the lentils have soaked, drain, then transfer to a food processor with the chile, garlic, ginger, and a pinch of salt. Blitz until smooth. Squeeze as much water from the zucchini as you can, return to a dry bowl, and combine with the lentil mix and cilantro. Heat a little oil in a nonstick skillet until hot. Fry tablespoons of the mix until golden, about 4 minutes, then flip and continue cooking until the other side is also golden. Repeat with the remaining batter. Makes 8.

Roast red pepper and lentil soup

4 red bell peppers, halved and seeded
2 garlic cloves, chopped
Olive oil
1 onion, finely chopped
1 fennel, finely chopped
1 carrot, finely chopped
1 tsp. smoked paprika
1 cup red split lentils
2 tbsp. tomato paste
1 tbsp. harissa
4 cups broth
Cilantro leaves, to serve

A chunky, earthy, smoky soup to serve with good, crusty bread.

Preheat the oven to 400°F. Put the bell peppers on a baking sheet, scatter over the garlic, drizzle with oil, and season. Roast for 25-30 minutes, until soft. Set aside to cool, then remove the skin and chop very finely. Meanwhile, in a heavy-bottomed saucepan, cook the onion, fennel, and carrot in a little oil until soft. Add the paprika, stir for a minute, then tip in the lentils, tomato paste, harissa, and broth, and simmer for 15 minutes. Add the chopped bell peppers and continue simmering until the lentils are cooked, 5-10 minutes. Season and eat topped with cilantro. Serves 4.

Capers

These olive-green pickled flower buds, which grow on the caper bush found all over the Mediterranean, are a real pantry workhorse. The smaller buds are considered the best, with nonpareil capers being the smallest, coming in at less than ¼ inch (the widely available capotes are around ⅜ inch). Once pickled in vinegar or salted, use these tiny, briny things to add bite and bring sauces, salads, pastas, fish dishes, and pizza toppings to life, or to counterbalance creamy or rich sauces. Capers will keep for months in the refrigerator but be sure to rinse them and pat dry before using.

PAIR WITH	Smoked salmon, white fish, mackerel, tuna, anchovy, chicken, eggs, cauliflower, eggplant, potatoes, celeriac, green beans, zucchini, tomatoes, artichoke, lemon, parsley, olives, mustard, honey, and harissa.
TRANSFORM	Frying capers in oil is a gamechanger; they open up like blooming flowers, with a salty, crunchy result, ideal for topping dips, roast veg, or broths.
HACK	Once open, be sure the capers are submerged in liquid before storing in the refrigerator.

Zucchini and caper gnocchi

2 tbsp. olive oil

2 garlic cloves, finely chopped

1 large zucchini, grated

14 oz. fresh gnocchi

Small handful basil, torn

Small handful parsley, chopped

Large handful arugula, chopped

1 tbsp. capers, drained, rinsed, and chopped

Half a lemon, zested and juiced

2½ tbsp. toasted pine nuts

Light, vibrant, and fresh, you could also top this salsa verde-esque gnocchi with pumpkin seeds, if you don't have pine nuts.

Heat the oil in a large saucepan, then fry the garlic for a minute. Add the zucchini, a big pinch of salt, and a good grind of black pepper, and fry until softened—about 5 minutes. Meanwhile, cook the gnocchi according to the package instructions, then drain, retaining a little cooking water.

Stir the herbs, arugula, capers, and lemon zest and juice into the zucchini, followed by the gnocchi plus a splash of cooking water. Top with the toasted pine nuts. Serves 2.

Lemony green beans and capers

1 heaping tbsp. capers, drained, rinsed, and chopped

Half a lemon, zested and juiced

2 tbsp. olive oil

2 cups fine green beans

These light and bright beans make the perfect bed for escalopes or umami-rich grilled mushrooms.

In a large bowl, combine the capers, lemon zest and juice, and olive oil, and season with black pepper. Bring a saucepan of salted water to a boil, add the beans, and cook until tender—about 3 minutes. Drain, rinse under cold water, then transfer to the large bowl. Toss to coat the beans with the dressing. Serves 3-4

Caper chimichurri

2 large handfuls parsley, finely chopped (stalks and all)

1 tbsp. dried oregano

2 tbsp. capers, drained and rinsed

1 shallot, chopped

2 garlic cloves, finely chopped

Good pinch of red pepper flakes

1 tsp. smoked paprika

1 tbsp. sherry vinegar

2 tbsp. extra virgin olive oil

Here, I've subbed in capers in this classic South American herb sauce, which balances grilled meats perfectly.

Put the first eight ingredients in a food processor with a pinch of salt and blend to a paste. Tip into a bowl and stir through the olive oil. Serves 4-6.

Baked squash caponata

1 butternut squash, peeled and cut into chunks

2 red onions, cut into chunks

3 garlic cloves, crushed

¼ cup pitted olives

3 tbsp. olive oil

1 can (14½ oz.) plum tomatoes

2 tbsp. red wine vinegar

2 tbsp. capers, drained, rinsed, and chopped

3 tbsp. raisins

Large handful parsley, chopped

This really benefits from a rest to allow the flavors to mingle, so leave for 15 minutes or so before serving.

Preheat the oven to 425°F. Put the squash, onions, garlic, olives, oil, and some seasoning on a baking sheet. Roast for 30 minutes, then tip in the tomatoes, combine, and return to the oven for 15 minutes. Meanwhile, in a large bowl, combine the vinegar, capers, raisins, and parsley, then tip in the veg and combine. Taste and adjust the seasoning if need be. Serves 4.

Fish parcels with lemon and capers

1–2 tbsp. olive oil

1 shallot, finely chopped

2 tbsp. capers, drained and rinsed

Splash of white wine

Squeeze of lemon juice

2 fillets of sole

This quick and simple dressing partners perfectly with white fish.

Preheat the oven to 400°F. Put 1 tablespoon olive oil in a saucepan, then cook the shallot until soft. Add the capers and a splash of wine, then bubble for a few minutes. Add a good squeeze of lemon juice, and season. Put each piece of fish on a 20-inch square of parchment paper, then top with the shallot mix. Drizzle with a little oil, then fold the edges of the paper, and scrunch together to seal. Roast for 10-12 minutes, until the fish is cooked through. Serves 2.

Pomegranate molasses

This thick, sticky, tart Middle Eastern syrup is made by slowly reducing pomegranate juice (with or without added sugar), resulting in a subtle, mellow sourness. And a little can really bring depth and complexity to dressings for salads (in lieu of balsamic vinegar in, say, vinaigrette, maybe with some sumac), sauces for meat (think meatballs), plus a sweet-sour vibe to stews or roasted veg, and a hit of acidity when drizzled into dips. Pomegranate molasses is incredibly versatile, and is just as pleasing in sweet dishes, being particularly well suited to drizzling over fruit salads or on top of a panna cotta—just be sure there are some fresh pomegranate seeds as well.

PAIR WITH	Roast chicken, beef, ham, halloumi, feta, pumpkin, beet, red cabbage, kale, carrot, eggplant, Brussels sprouts, tomatoes, citrus, fresh pomegranate, figs, plums, dates, mint, tahini, walnuts, quinoa, and bulgur wheat.
TRANSFORM	Near-empty bottle? Pour in some hot water, swirl it around, then pour over a roast chicken about 10 minutes before it's done cooking. You'll be left with a wonderful sticky glaze.
HACK	A little syrup goes a long way to creating a sweet-sour cocktail. Try adding to a pomegranate fizz, or use to dip the rims of glasses in (before you coat in salt/sugar) for a margarita.

Honey roast figs

1 tbsp. pomegranate molasses

1 tbsp. golden honey

Half a lemon, zested and juiced

2 sprigs thyme, leaves chopped

4 figs, halved

A quick and easy breakfast or dessert. Serve topped with toasted pistachios and yogurt.

In a bowl, combine the pomegranate molasses, honey, lemon zest and juice, thyme, a pinch of salt, and a splash of water. Add the figs, combine, and set aside while you preheat the oven to 400°F. Tip the figs into a baking dish (making sure they're sitting cut-side up) and bake for 30 minutes. Serves 2-4.

Shredded sprout and apple salad with barberries

3 tbsp. olive oil

1 lemon, juiced

1 tsp. golden honey

1 tsp. sumac

1 tbsp. pomegranate molasses

2 sprigs thyme, leaves chopped

5½ cups Brussels sprouts, shredded

1 apple, cut into sticks

2 scallions, sliced

2 tbsp. barberries

Barberries, which are small, dried berries from Iran, bring a tangy edge. Otherwise, zante currants soaked in a little lemon juice will add similar sharpness.

In a large bowl, combine the oil, lemon juice, honey, sumac, pomegranate molasses, thyme, and some seasoning. Add the remaining ingredients and combine. Serves 4, as a side.

Shallot tarte tatin

11¼ oz. circle puff pastry

2 tbsp. olive oil

6 banana shallots (1¼ lb.), halved

2 tbsp. balsamic vinegar

2 tbsp. golden honey

1 tbsp. pomegranate molasses

2 sprigs thyme, leaves picked

2 sprigs rosemary, leaves picked

If you don't have an ovenproof skillet, transfer the cooked shallots to a pie dish before topping with the pastry.

Roll the puff pastry into a circle about ¾ inch larger than your ovenproof skillet; put in the refrigerator while you get on with the rest. Heat the oil in the skillet, then add the shallots and cook for 5 minutes. Add the balsamic, honey, pomegranate molasses, herbs, and some salt and pepper. Cook for another 10 minutes, then arrange the shallots cut-side down in the pan; cool a little. Preheat the oven to 400°F. Lay the pastry over the shallots, tucking it down around the edges. Prick a couple of times with a fork, then bake for 25-30 minutes, until puffed up and golden. Remove from the oven and leave to cool for 5 minutes before putting a plate or board over the pan, and carefully flipping over. Serves 6.

Beets, walnuts, and pomegranate with harissa yogurt

2 beets, cut into chunks
1 tbsp. olive oil
2 tbsp. pomegranate molasses
2 garlic cloves, crushed
¾ cup walnuts, chopped
Large handful dill, chopped
Seeds from half a pomegranate
1 lemon, zested and juiced
¾ cup yogurt
1 tbsp. rose harissa

Roasting beet brings out its wonderful sweetness, which would also work nicely eaten with labneh.

Preheat the oven to 400°F. Put the beets on a baking sheet. In a bowl, mix the olive oil, the pomegranate molasses, garlic, and some salt and pepper. Tip over the beets and combine. Roast until cooked through—start checking after an hour. Remove from the oven and toss through the chopped walnuts, dill, and pomegranate seeds. In a bowl, combine the lemon zest and 1 teaspoon juice, the yogurt, and harissa. Serve alongside the beets. Serves 4, as a side.

Pomegranate fattoush

2–3 tbsp. olive oil
2 pitta, torn into chunks
½ tbsp. pomegranate molasses
1 tsp. sumac
Half a lemon, juiced
1 garlic clove, crushed
3 small cucumbers, chopped
2¼ cups tomatoes, cut into chunks
4 scallions, sliced
¾ cup radishes, sliced
1 small head romaine lettuce, chopped
Small bunch parsley, chopped
Small bunch mint, chopped
Seeds from half a pomegranate

The pitta, which soaks up all the flavors, is undoubtedly the best part of this Middle Eastern salad—so don't scrimp.

Heat a little oil in a skillet, then add the pitta chunks and fry until golden; drain on paper towels. In a lidded glass jar, add two tablespoons olive oil, the pomegranate molasses, sumac, lemon juice, garlic, and some seasoning, and shake. In a serving bowl, add the remaining ingredients and pitta chunks, pour over the dressing, and toss. Serves 4.

Recipe index

A

Aji verde 131

Aloo tikki 158

Anchovy and lemon salsa 123

Artichoke and lemon pasta 42

Artichoke panzanella 43

Artichoke, pea, and spelt salad 43

Artichoke skillet pie 42

B

Bacon and pineapple hash 39

Baked eggs with avocado 31

Baked gnocchi with sausage and kale 30

Baked honey feta with tomatoes 94

Baked kimchi and kale rice with eggs 118

Baked leek and bacon rice 146

Baked lemon lentils and kale 162

Baked pea falafel 158

Baked polenta with tomatoes 54

Baked squash caponata 167

Balsamic and mustard pork chops 142

Banana and oat pancakes 86

Beet burgers 143

Beets, walnuts, and pomegranate with harissa yogurt 171

Black bean and sweet potato pie 139

Black bean, tahini, and chile dip 139

Blackberry, apple, and thyme crumble bars 87

Broccoli and anchovy gratin 122

Broccoli and black bean noodles 138

Broccoli Reuben pan bake 131

Brothy harissa couscous and chicken 154

Brussels sprout and anchovy tart 122

C

Cacio e pepe butter beans 34

Cannellini and carrot burgers 47

Caper chimichurri 166

Carrot cake overnight oats 86

Carrot top gremolata 71

Cashew and date energy balls 106

Cauliflower and mushroom Bolognese 78

Cauliflower, carrot, and spinach dal 98

Cauliflower toad 143

Celeriac and apple remoulade 131

Cheese and chutney English muffins 74

Cherry and basil friands 110

Cherry and coconut crumble 110

Cherry and ricotta cake 111

Cherry and rosemary shrub 110

Chicken kale Caesar 130

Chicken, leek, and bean pan bake 46

Chickpeas alla vodka 62

Chickpea pancakes with Swiss chard and salted ricotta 159

Chocolate and coffee crinkle cookies 82

Chocolate drizzled ginger madeleines 83

Chocolate, miso, and pecan cookies 22

Chorizo pearl barley with a fried egg 151

Coconut rice 98

Corn bread with roast tomatoes 19

Coronation chickpeas 74

Couscous kedgeree with chickpeas 155

Crab and mango rice noodles 126

Crab cocktail 130

Creamy kimchi udon 118

Crispy haddock and watercress bread rolls 71

E

Eggplant polpette 90

F

Fasolakia (Greek green beans) 30

Fish cakes 50

Fish parcels with lemon and capers 167

Flatbread with romesco, leeks, and ricotta 59

Flourless chocolate, pear, and hazelnut cake 83

Fried pineapple rice 39

G

Garlicky cannellini mash 46

Gildas 123

Gingery carrot and rice soup 146

Gluten-free bechamel 159

Grapefruit polenta cake 54

Green goddess tuna sandwich 134

Greens and bean crumble 47

H

Harissa and fennel butter beans with herby yogurt 35

Harissa cheese straws 67

Harissa frittata with herbs and feta 67

Harissa squash, carrot, and chickpea pan bake 67

Hazelnut pesto 107

Herb and pistachio pilaf 146

Herby leeks and eggs 142

Herby lentil soup 90

Honey and pistachio cakes 95

Honey and rosemary roast nuts 94

Honey-mustard sausages with sweet potato 94

Honey roast figs 170

Honey roast grape and goat cheese toast 95

Huevos rancheros-style scramble 138

K

Kimchi and grilled cheese 119

Kimchi bubble and squeak 119

Kimchi pancakes 118

L

Leek, sage, and walnut tart 107

Lentil lasagne 91

Lentil stuffed sweet potatoes 163

Lemon and green olive spaghetti 102

Lemon, chickpea, and parsley orecchiette 63

Lemony green beans and capers 166

M

Mango chutney paneer with spinach 75

Marinated butter beans 35

Mini carrot and pineapple cakes 39

Miso, asparagus, and pea risotto 22

Miso eggplant fries 23

Miso deviled eggs 23

Miso mushroom sausage rolls 70

Moussaka bowls 91

Mushroom and bok choi noodle soup 79

Mushroom and spinach spelt 79
Mushroom broth 79
Mushroom chili 82

N

Noodles in ginger and turmeric broth with Swiss chard 126

O

Oat and rosemary crackers 86
Olive and sun-dried tomato farinata 158

P

Packed lunch couscous in a jar 154
Parsnip, apple, and barley soup 150
Pasta e fagioli 46
PBJ yogurt parfait 115

Pea and butter bean dip 34
Pea and potato pakoras 74
Pea, bean, and broccoli couscous with pistou 154
Peanut butter crispy bars 114
Peanut noodles with smacked cucumber 115
Pearl barley with feta and roast mushrooms 151
Pearl barley pudding with pears and honey 151
Pearl barley, smoked mackerel and beet salad 150
Peppercorn mushrooms 78
Pineapple and ginger upside-down cake 38
Pineapple and green bean curry 38
Plum brown betty 71
Polenta and rosemary roast potatoes 55
Polenta fries 55

Polenta pastry 55
Pomegranate fattoush 171
Preserved lemonade 102
Preserved lemon drizzle cake 103
Preserved lemon hasselback potatoes 103
Preserved lemon vinaigrette 102
Prune and oat scones 87
Pumpkin seed butter 106

Q

Quick-pickled cherries 111

R

Ramen pancake 127
Raspberry and coconut ice popsicles 98
Red miso and shiitake ramen 23
Red pepper and mushroom quesadillas 58

Red pepper and walnut pesto 58
Roast fennel, lentils, and salsa verde 91
Roast red pepper and lentil soup 163
Roast red pepper rice 59
Roast spiced chickpeas 62
Roast tomatoes and anchovies 122

S

Sardine, celery, and lemon salad 50
Sardine linguine with pangrattato 51
Sardine puttanesca and polenta 50
Sardine Reuben 51
Shallot tarte tatin 170
Shredded sprout and apple salad with barberries 170
Shrimp with peppers 58
Simple chocolate mousse 62
Soba noodle salad 127

Spanakopita zucchini boats 155

Spiced hot chocolate 83

Spiced shepherd's pie with butter bean mash 34

Spicy peanut sauce 114

Spinach and artichoke dip 42

Squash, sage, and chestnut rice 147

Sriracha baked salmon 14

Sriracha garlic bread 15

Sriracha mayo 14

Sriracha pickled cucumbers 15

Sriracha sprouts 14

Sticky harissa chicken 66

Sticky mango chicken and potatoes 75

Stuffed harissa tomatoes 66

Sushi salad bowl 147

Sweet corn and black bean nachos 18

Sweet corn and black bean taco salad 139

Sweet corn and peanut curry 99

Sweet corn drop scones 19

Sweet corn slaw 19

Sweet corn, spinach, and feta phyllo triangles 18

Sweet potato, coconut, and lime soup 99

Sweet potato, peanut, and spinach stew 114

T

Tahini and chocolate banana bread 27

Tahini butter 26

Tahini, date, and cinnamon porridge 26

Tahini granola 106

Tahini-mustard dressing 142

Tomato and coconut lentils 162

Tomato and feta orzo 31

Tomato chana dal 30

Tahini yogurt chickpeas with pickled red onion 63

Tuna, crispy chickpea, and radicchio salad 134

Tuna stuffed peppers 135

Tuna, tomato, and olive spaghetti 135

Tuna tortilla 134

U

Udon carbonara 127

W

Whipped tahini with squash and pine nuts 27

Z

Zucchini and caper gnocchi 166

Zucchini and lentil fritters 163

Zucchini, mint, and tahini soup 26

Zucchini parmigiana 70

Acknowledgments

Firstly, thank you for buying this book. Thank you to
the team at Skittledog and everyone involved in making
Pantry Genius, particularly Zara Larcombe for giving me
the opportunity, your guidance and bringing this vision
to life. To Virginia Brehaut, for your support, eye(s)
and keeping me on track. A big thank you to Agnieszka
Więckowska for the wonderful illustrations—you made
this book beautiful.

Special thanks to my mom, Jeannette, for testing recipes,
Alan and Tom for your appetite, even when eggplants were
involved, and to Penfold (the dog), for selflessly cleaning up
gratings of carrot and near-empty jars of peanut butter.

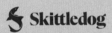 **Skittledog**

First published in the United Kingdom in 2024
by Skittledog, an imprint of Thames & Hudson Ltd,
181A High Holborn, London WC1V 7QX

Concept and layout © Thames & Hudson 2024

Text © Anna Berrill 2024
Illustrations © Agnieszka Więckowska 2024

All Rights Reserved. No part of this publication may be
reproduced or transmitted in any form or by any means,
electronic or mechanical, including photocopy, recording
or any other information storage and retrieval system,
without prior permission in writing from the publisher.

British Library Cataloging-in-Publication Data
A catalog record for this book is available from
the British Library

Distributed in North America by Abrams

ISBN 978-1-837-76043-5

Printed and bound in China by C&C Offset Printing Co., Ltd

Senior Editor: Virginia Brehaut
Designer: Megan van Staden
Production: Felicity Awdry

Be the first to know about our new releases, exclusive
content and author events by visiting:

skittledog.com
thamesandhudson.com
thamesandhudsonusa.com
thamesandhudson.com.au